'Agapi is the Goddess of GODS AND GODDESSES and you'll feel her love coming through these pages. Make this book your gift to yourself and everyone you love.'

– Michael J. Gelb, author of *DaVinci Decoded*

'Ms. Stassinopoulous, an actress turned psychologist turned motivational speaker and the sister of Arianna Huffington, intends to be a sort of Joseph Campbell and Linda Goodman of the OO's, a synthesis that gives her opinions a familiarly cozy and rather quaint 70's quality.'

– *The New York Times*

'This book helps us to experience the goddess archetypes in each of our lives. To me that is what has been missing in the modern-day world for both women and men.'

– *Shirley MacLaine*

Also by Agapi Stassinopoulos

Conversations with the Goddesses

GODS & GODDESSES IN LOVE

Getting the Life & Love That's Right For You

AGAPI STASSINOPOULOS

ROBSON BOOKS

This paperback edition first published in Great Britain in 2005 by
Robson Books, The Chrysalis Building, Bramley Road, London W10 6SP

An imprint of **Chrysalis** Books Group plc

First published in 2004 in the US by PARAVIEW POCKET BOOKS, a
division of Simon & Schuster, Inc., 1230 Avenue of the Americas, New
York, NY 10020

The author has made every reasonable effort to contact all copyright holders.
Any errors that may have occurred are inadvertent and anyone who for any
reason has not been contacted is invited to write to the publishers so that a
full acknowledgement may be made in subsequent editions of this work.

British Library Cataloguing in Publication Data
A catalogue record for this title is available from the British Library.

ISBN 1 86105 896 9

Cover design by Richard Mason
Interior design by Jaime Putorti

Printed and bound by Clays Ltd, Bungay, Suffolk

The Goddess Quiz, 'Which Goddess Are You?' by Eileen Livers and Agapi
Stassinopoulos; and The God Quiz, 'The Greek God Test' by Eileen Livers.
Adapted from iVillage.com, the number one Women's Website, with permission.

For Arianna, Christina and Isabella,
with all my love

CONTENTS

What's the good of a man
unless there is the glimpse of a god in him?
And what's the good of a woman
unless she is a glimpse of a goddess of some sort?

— D. H. LAWRENCE

PREFACE

What I have learned about the Gods and Goddesses of Greece I learned not through books but through personal experience. I was raised by parents who loved and adored me but whose unhappy and tumultuous marriage ended in separation when I was just twelve years old. They met just after World War II in Athens, Greece. My father, Costas, who published an underground newspaper during the German occupation of Greece, survived a year and a half in a concentration camp in Germany before returning to Greece at the end of the war. My mother, Elli, had joined the Red Cross and contributed to the war effort in her own way. My father was a seductive, commanding and romantic intellectual. My mother was a beautiful, strong, smart woman who described their first encounter as a cosmic attraction of body, mind and soul, and their time together as an odyssey.

During their love affair, my mother became pregnant with my sister and, of course, wanted to get married. But having survived his long ordeal as a prisoner in the camps, my father wanted his freedom and wasn't ready to settle down. My mother then decided to go to Switzerland to have her baby, and that pressure, as well as his sense of destiny, caused my father to marry her.

Soon enough, however, he started to rebel against the bonds of marriage. He hadn't had a chance to heal the psychological wounds inflicted during his concentration camp experience, nor did he have the resources to process such a trauma. He was simply incapable of dealing with the demands and responsibilities of a family. Despite his many talents and his brilliant mind, every business venture he touched withered. He loved to go out every night, but my mother had a small child at home and didn't want to go with him. So he went out on his own and then began having affairs and spending his evenings in nightclubs, drinking and gambling, all of which caused my mother tremendous pain, heartache and anger. In the midst of this turmoil, she became pregnant again and decided she couldn't possibly have another child.

She made an appointment to terminate the pregnancy, but on the scheduled day she and my father had a loving encounter in bed, and he persuaded her to keep the child, which was me. I think he knew in his heart that I was coming to bring him comfort and solace, which, in fact, I did all my life until the moment he died on May 11, 2000.

Throughout my life, I believed it was my responsibility to try to bridge the gap between my parents that prevented them from communicating their love for each other. As an innocent and sensitive child, I felt their pain but was helpless to do anything about it. Yet I tried in every way possible to bring them joy and to reunite them. My romantic ideal held that my parents should live happily ever after and love and care for each other, and that we should be a family again. Instead, there was anger, hurt and separation. However, I feel privileged to have witnessed a profound healing between them in the last year before they passed away, within three months of each other.

Despite the betrayal, anger and pain that coloured their relationship, the force of love that had initially brought them together never died. Their healing began when my father asked my mother to forgive him, which allowed her heart to open so that she could love him again. With that simple request he gave them both a great gift – he freed her spirit and liberated her heart.

My father was like the god Zeus, king of Olympus, with aspects of turbulent Poseidon, ruler of the seas, and brooding Hades, god of the underworld. Even as a married man, he continued to romance other women and believed he had the prerogative to be with any woman he chose. One morning, after he returned from one of his escapades, my mother asked him where he had been. His reply was perhaps the most Zeus-like statement ever made: 'I forbid you to interfere in my personal life.' In shutting her out from any discussion and resolution, he ultimately drove my mother to take her two daughters and leave. She would often blame herself for having married him and would find consolation in the fact that he had gifted her with two daughters, my sister and myself.

To me, my father was the god I adored, and I forgave him unconditionally. I was always able to see beyond his behaviour to the essence of his soul, which was the deep tender soul of a poet. Even as a child I knew intuitively that as a concentration camp survivor he had suffered a great psychic wound and that his addictive behaviour was his way of trying to release his pain. He was expressing the dark side of his soul, the Hades who resides in our unconscious and rules the darkness in our lives – our depressions, anxieties and grief. My father didn't know that he was profoundly depressed and tried to alleviate his depression through his addictions.

Although his behaviour hurt my mother tremendously, I knew that my father was the one who desperately needed my love. The night before he died, he said to me, as he had said many times before, 'You are my comforter.' I think, ultimately, there is nothing more rewarding or noble than to bring comfort to another person, and the greatest surrender of all is to also learn to receive comfort from another. Then we have heaven on earth.

My mother's life with my father was filled with challenges and betrayals. For twelve years she was the betrayed Hera, goddess of marriage, unable to do anything but endure. She felt powerless in a marriage that was oppressive. But then she discovered her powerful Demeter archetype, nurturer and goddess of the earth, which gave her the strength to leave him, take her children with her and raise us herself.

My parents were never divorced, and although my mother was a beautiful woman, she never had another man in her life. She bestowed all her creativity and devotion on her daughters. All my values I received from her. 'Develop your skills and gifts so you can become independent,' she used to say. She wanted to make sure that we would rely on ourselves and not on a man. And when it came to the qualities I should look for in a man, she stressed responsibility. Sex, she would say to me, was a sacred act and should always be experienced with love. However, my mother had locked away her own Aphrodite, and as my own life progressed, I discovered that I had taken on many of her personality traits, keeping men at a distance out of fear not to repeat her patterns. I had to learn for myself how to release and give expression to the love goddess in me and allow her to infuse my life.

My parents taught me the greatest lesson there is – that even in the midst of betrayal, pain, anger, loss and turbulence, there is also an inescapable driving force that is love. I believe we are meant to live with love as our guiding principle at all times. We need to understand that even in our aloneness we are never truly alone, that we can and should be loved for who we are, and that we don't have to change ourselves in order to conform to someone else's expectations. Through relationships we learn about the mystery of loving and we learn to heal our wounds so we can experience joy in life on a daily basis. And, most important of all, we learn to open our hearts unconditionally to another person. As we reveal ourselves to another, we reveal ourselves to ourselves. We learn about the most lasting relationship of all – the relationship with our own soul.

In classical Greek drama, the *deus ex machina* was the deity who arrived at the end of the play to settle any unresolved entanglements of plot through divine intervention. For modern goddesses and gods, the *deus ex machina* to settle the entangled plots of our lives lies in the archetypal stories of the residents of Mount Olympus. By taking matters into our own hands – rather than relying on the whims of fate – and taking responsibility for creating the relationship we want, we become our own *deus ex machina*.

Chapter 1

THE GODS AND GODDESSES
ARE ALIVE WITHIN YOU

Everything is full of Gods.

– THALES

T hree thousand years ago, my Greek ancestors tried to identify the forces playing themselves out in human nature and created the eight gods and seven goddesses of Olympus, giving each of them a name and a story. Each one exemplifies an authentic pattern of feminine or masculine human nature. These gods and goddesses have fascinated me since my early years. Fearless, magical, flawed yet awesome, they have been with me throughout my life's journey. They were with me when I first fell in love, as I discovered how to express my gifts and develop qualities I didn't know I had, as I learned to build boundaries and turn inward for my source of happiness, and as I moved into pivotal events that would shape my life today.

In writing my first book, *Conversations with the Goddesses*, I embraced the seven goddess archetypes and learned to bring them down off their pedestals into our everyday life. I used them to fulfil my passion, which has been to inspire women to become all that they can be and create their own lives. Yet as my work evolved, the gods kept nagging me; they wanted to be sure I didn't forget them. As I began to focus my attention on them, I saw how they play in the psyches of the men I know, and men in society and history. I saw how the goddesses and the gods go together. In their myths we see them drawn together into perfectly imperfect unions – which is exactly how these relationships are designed to be. The myths show us our own relationships played out on the big screen of Olympus.

In ancient times, there were no therapists, no relationship workshops, no dating services and no divorce lawyers. Instead there were the myths, the stories of these gods and goddesses. Many centuries later, the Swiss psychologist Carl Jung called these deities 'archetypes', which means 'ancient types' in Greek. He identified the gods and goddesses as part of the collective unconscious, and pointed out how they make up the software of our psyche. These archetypes live within each man and woman, and the stories of their relationships and notorious adventures on Mount Olympus, as well as here on earth, provide a basis for understanding human personalities and behaviour.

In their stories, we recognise familiar scenarios. Zeus is unfaithful to Hera as he pursues liaisons with other goddesses and nymphs. She becomes angry and vengeful and ultimately leaves him to find herself. Aphrodite enters into an arranged marriage with Hephaestus and then, driven by eros, has an affair with his brother, Ares, as well as with other gods, demigods and mortals. Athena remains a virgin and bonds with men as their protector, while Artemis has nothing to do with men and prefers the company of women. Apollo is constantly experiencing unrequited love. Persephone is raped and abducted by Hades, god of the underworld, and ends up marrying him. Demeter sleeps with Zeus, has one daughter, then moves on to become a devoted single mother. Unlike the fairy tales in which everyone ends up living happily ever after, the Greek myths teach us that, in reality, relationships bring friction.

Each of us is born with a predominant archetype that is our driving force and directs our actions and choices. Yet each of us also contains all of the archetypes, and at different times in our lives we may favour one over another. We have all the gods and goddesses in us, but in differing degrees of intensity – some stronger, some weaker, some in the foreground, some in the background. A particular god dominates our lives at a particular stage only to retreat when we move on to a different stage. For example, a woman might have a strong desire to be married. That is her Hera speaking. When she feels the calling to have children, that is her Demeter tugging on her. And once her children are grown and independent, she may feel the urge to find meaningful work. This is her Athena stepping forward. She might suddenly awaken to her Aphrodite and want to have an affair or refuel her marriage with a new eros. Or she may feel a yearning to serve, to give back, to follow an inner path of spirit; that is the Hestia principle governing her.

The archetypes play themselves out through us. It is easy to get caught in those patterns. We find ourselves making certain choices without really knowing why. For instance, a Persephone woman may find herself getting involved in relationships that are destructive. Or an Athena woman may want a relationship, but feels too caught in the work ethic and is disconnected from her body to open up to love. Both of them are caught up in their myths.

Who is running the show?

As we become familiar with the archetypes, we begin to see the unconscious patterns that act themselves out in us. Then we can start to make wiser choices, based on what our real needs are. We gradually discover that the archetypes are here to serve us; that we can direct the archetypes and we can use them as needed. They become our tools in creating the life we want. To use my mother's favourite word, we become 'autonomous', a word that comes from the Greek and means a 'law unto one's self'. In other words, we become an independent thinker.

To be in a healthy, heartfelt relationship requires a lot of attention, care, commitment and hard work of the heart. Most of us have to unlearn a lot of our imbedded beliefs, and no one hands us a manual. However, the archetypes provide extraordinary clues. Why are some women more drawn to successful, powerful men, while others prefer the creative type? Why does one woman look for a compatible yet independent companion while another woman prefers a man who is dependent on her? Our dominant archetype shapes the choices we make about a partner. As you come to understand those archetypal patterns, you learn how they tend to operate in a relationship, and begin to consciously direct the way you interact.

You need not remain a prisoner of your archetype; you can always draw on your nondominant archetypes as allies. For example, if you are an Aphrodite quarrelling with your Ares partner, there is no better ally than Athena's wisdom to help you find your way to a resolution, and Hestia's steady presence can guide you back to what really matters in your relationship. We never have to be victims wondering why we don't have enough love or the right kind of love in our lives. If you were to say to yourself: the personal relationship – or lack of one – I have right now is exactly what I want, it might reveal to you a powerful piece of your inner puzzle. When we truly believe that we deserve to be loved, cherished, and supported as who we really are, we can attract the person who can do that for us.

In the next chapter you will find two quizzes that will help you identify your dominant and secondary archetypes, as well as the primary and secondary archetypes of the man in your life – or the man you might be looking for. The quizzes also provide an overview of all the feminine and masculine types.

In the remainder of this book you will find a description of each woman with her particular goddess archetype, showing how that goddess's personality and story influence the psyche of the woman, and highlighting her strengths and vulnerabilities. I then describe the woman's compatible male partner in terms of his god archetype and myth, followed by how these two archetypes play themselves out in a relationship, the patterns that might surface and suggestions as to how the couple can best work with these patterns. For each goddess, I also include a story of an actual modern couple that fits those archetypes. (The names and locations of the real people are changed to protect their privacy, except in the case of Gay and Katie Hendricks near the end of the book.)

I have paired each goddess with a god – or in Aphrodite's case, with two gods! – based on what their myths tell us. Such archetypal relationships have the quality of a template; they have been repeated and played out, with minor variations, throughout history in both fiction and life. In some cases, such as pairing Hestia with Hermes, I've based the match on relationships I have seen and on the qualities that each archetype can bring to the relationship. Of course other combinations are possible because we have other archetypes working in us. You might be an Artemis woman dating a Zeus man. You might discover, for instance, that you are actually drawn to his Apollo aspect, which is secondary, and you find his Zeus aspect overpowering, reminding you of your father. The more you understand all the archetypes, the better you can see how your relationship reflects them.

If there is one characteristic that defines all the gods, it is self-confidence. They acted boldly, courageously, fully embodying who they were, flaws and all. They were free of judgment and guilt about what they did. This is a great role model for us. They show us how to be generous with ourselves, act fearlessly, unleash our creativity, and claim who we are. Most of all, they show us how to be alive.

As Joseph Campbell said, 'People say that what we're all seeking is a meaningful life. I don't think that's what we're really seeking. I think that what we are seeking is an experience of being alive, so that our life experiences on the purely physical plane will have resonances within our own innermost being and reality, so that we actually feel the rapture of being alive.' We are so engaged in doing things to achieve purposes of outer value that we forget that the inner value, the rapture that is associated with being alive, is what it's all about. As he said, 'Myth helps you to put your mind in touch with this experience of being alive.'

As you befriend the gods and goddesses, converse with them. Let them speak to you, let them bring you information about yourself and your relationships, and use them to create the life you want.

Chapter 2

YOUR GODDESS (AND HIS GOD) – THE QUIZZES

Quiz Instructions

The two quizzes in this chapter will help you discover your predominant goddess archetype and the predominant god archetype of the man in your life. Read each question and choose the answer that seems right for you. Then add up how many of each letter you have marked. See the scoring chart at the end of each quiz for the answers, then read about your archetype, and his, in the brief descriptions that follow.

The Goddess Quiz

1. What is the most important thing in your life?
    a. Marriage
    b. Serving others
    c. Romance and passion
    d. Career
    e. Independence
    f. Finding myself
    g. Children

2. What do you want most out of marriage?
    a. An equal partnership
    b. The opportunity to create a warm, nurturing home life
    c. Passion – without it, what is there?
    d. Friendship – it's the key to a long-lasting relationship
    e. I'm not sure I will get married
    f. A spiritual partnership
    g. Children – I can't wait to be a mother

3. Your ideal life partner is:
    a. Self-confident – someone who would never feel threatened by me
    b. Service-oriented – someone who strives to do for others
    c. Passionate – someone who is as loving and sexual as I am
    d. Intelligent – someone with whom I can discuss all kinds of interesting topics
    e. Independent – someone who believes partners can have their own lives

    f. Mature and successful – someone whose position in the world is impressive

    g. Stable and protective – someone who can provide for me and our family

4. When it comes to sex, you:

    a. Enjoy the give-and-take that leads to mutual pleasure

    b. Can take it or leave it – you feel fulfilled without it, as long as there is love in your relationship

    c. Are easily aroused and thoroughly enjoy sex – with a desired partner, of course

    d. Usually feel awkward and disconnected from your body – it's hard to let go of what's going on in your head and let your body enjoy the experience

    e. May seem aloof and withdrawn at first, but once you relax and get into it, anything can happen!

    f. Find it to be a powerful, almost transforming experience

    g. Enjoy pleasing your partner but don't usually focus on having your own needs met

5. On a typical (child-free) Saturday afternoon, you would most likely be found:

    a. Doing something with your partner that he enjoys or volunteering at your favourite charity organisation

    b. Gardening or doing housework

    c. Shopping or visiting an art museum with friends, or getting a massage

    d. Attending a lecture series or author reading, or curled up with a good book

e. Doing something athletic outdoors, such as hiking or sailing

f. Reading your horoscope, meditating, or participating in some other New Age practice

g. In the kitchen – cooking and possibly preparing to entertain at home that evening

6. If you were to throw a luncheon for your friends, whose names would be on your guest list?

a. The wives and girlfriends of my mate's friends

b. Women I've met while doing volunteer work in the community

c. A fun group of girlfriends I feel comfortable sharing everything with

d. Mostly men friends – I have more of them than female friends

e. A few very close, carefully chosen friends

f. A small group of close friends with whom I share an almost spiritual connection

g. Women who have children the same age(s) as mine

7. A friend calls to invite you to a party next Saturday night. You:

a. Attend and stay close to your partner – you two tend to mingle together

b. Find a way to get out of it – you'd rather spend the time at home

c. Can't wait to go – you love to be the life of the party

d. Go and get caught up in a conversation about current events, politics, or work

e. Mingle freely, never spending too much time with any one person or group

f. Go and get involved in a heavy conversation with one person

g. Help the host or hostess in the kitchen and make sure everyone is having a good time

8. Which profession most appeals to you?
    a. Head of volunteer organisation
    b. Nurse or social worker
    c. Clothing designer, actress/singer, public relations person
    d. Lawyer or business executive
    e. Adventure guide or camp leader
    f. Psychotherapist
    g. Restaurant owner or chef/caterer

9. If you could create your dream home, what would it be like?
    a. A beautiful large house with gardens in an elegant neighbourhood
    b. A house or apartment that is like a sanctuary, protected and private
    c. A penthouse apartment decorated in gold tones, rich colours and fabrics
    d. A modern, functional apartment in New York or another fast-paced, stimulating city
    e. A house with plenty of land around it, near a park or other open spaces
    f. An artist's loft in New York City where I can be creative
    g. A suburban home that has a large kitchen and where people feel comfortable coming to visit

10. Which of the following activities would recharge you the most?
    a. Socialising with friends or attending a social event
    b. Doing volunteer work
    c. Shopping, especially for clothes
    d. Going to a bookstore or spending time reading
    e. Taking a walk outdoors
    f. Meditating or otherwise spending some quiet time alone with your thoughts
    g. Cooking for family and friends

11. Your clothing closet is filled mostly with:
    a. Simple, classic styles that allow you to look put-together but not fussy or trendy
    b. A hodgepodge of items purchased without much thought or planning
    c. Clothes that mould to your body in soft, luxurious fabrics
    d. Outfits you feel confident in and know will make a positive impression
    e. Exercise clothing, jeans and other comfortable, casual clothes
    f. Artsy, somewhat eccentric items
    g. Simple, comfortable items good for lounging in at home and playing with children

12. Which of the following statements is most true for you?
    a. I like my body best when I know my partner finds me attractive
    b. My outward appearance matters less to me than how I feel on the inside
    c. My body makes me feel sexy and attractive

d. I don't spend much time thinking about my body
e. I take care of my body so that I can exercise and
be active
f. I am struggling to make peace with my body
g. What I like best about my body is its ability to
bear children

Scoring

Add up the number of a's, b's, c's, d's, e's, f's and g's
you have chosen and match the answers with the goddesses
as shown below. A brief sketch of each goddess archetype
follows.

Answers	Your total	Goddesses
A	1	Hera
B	2	Hestia
C	2	Aphrodite
D	0	Athena
E	3	Artemis
F	1	Persephone
G	3	Demeter

The letter you have chosen the most represents the goddess
who primarily rules your personality. If you have the same
number of two or more letters, several goddesses influence
your personality evenly. No matter which goddess or goddesses rule your personality, be sure to pay attention to the

other goddesses, who influence you to a lesser degree, as well. Every woman has aspects of all seven goddesses in her personality. To achieve a healthy balance, you need to integrate characteristics of each goddess in your life.

a. Hera

If you possess many of Hera's qualities, you tend to find fulfilment in relationships and look on marriage as a permanent union. In marriage you feel no sense of frustration or resentment because you are an equal partner with your spouse. You are confident and have no trouble asserting your authority in and out of the relationship. You seek men who are self-confident and successful, because you are comfortable with the concept that you can be fulfiled through him (and him through you). As long as your partner honours the marriage as much as you do and appreciates you, you will be happy. If he doesn't, you must concentrate on your own growth and discover an identity independent of him.

b. Hestia

If you embody the qualities of Hestia, you understand the value of having your own sacred place, whether it's an actual room or simply a time of day when you free your mind of busy thoughts and experience peace. While home is your sanctuary, you are at home with yourself wherever you are and no matter who you are with. You know that the meaning of your life springs from your spiritual centre. This brings you a great sense of security. You do not crave attention or material possessions; you nurture your friends and family with your unconditional love.

c. Aphrodite

If you are ruled mostly by Aphrodite, your femininity and passionate spirit are the controlling forces in your life. You tend to be charismatic and self-assured, comfortable with your body, and unrestrained sexually. Men are drawn to you like bees to flowers; this satisfies your erotic nature. However, you tend not to form permanent attachments with lovers because you value your sexual freedom, and this may leave you feeling lonely and even depleted once a relationship ends. To find and form a more lasting relationship, you need to add more of the goddess Hera to your life.

d. Athena

If you are ruled by Athena, you are bright-eyed, shrewd, resourceful and inventive. With friends, you are the wise counsellor – always ready with an empowering message. You believe strongly that women can accomplish anything men can. No wonder you put so much time into your career! Athena women tend to be ruled by their heads, not by their hearts. You carefully guard your intimate side, protecting your emotions and vulnerability. If you want to awaken your unexpressed womanliness, you'll have to use the same passion you apply to your intellectual achievements. It's important that you work to integrate your strong masculine side with your feminine side – bringing together your strength and your vulnerability, your creativity and your caring, your intelligence and your imagination. Allow your aspects of the goddesses Hestia and Aphrodite to help you do this.

e. Artemis

If you are ruled by Artemis, you are an independent spirit and belong to no one but yourself. Your body is vibrant, your attitude robust and your manner vigorous and alive. You are driven by physical rather than mental energy. You feel complete without a man in your life and would never compromise your essential nature for a romantic partner. You are skilled at establishing personal boundaries and enter into relationships on your own terms – in short, you can take care of yourself. This attitude may at times put men off.

f. Persephone

If you exemplify the qualities of Persephone, you have an ethereal, otherworldly air about you and are highly creative. Your youthful spirit shines through no matter what your age. You are also familiar with either emotional or physical loss. This experience has forced you to face the dark, unenlightened side of yourself and transform yourself into a stronger, more independent, more accepting and more compassionate person. It may have also led you down a spiritual path and moved you to place great emphasis on inner calm and on close connections with friends. You are capable of embracing, integrating and accepting difficult experiences. Because of this skill, you offer others the gift of empathy – you understand what others have been through.

g. Demeter

If you fit the Demeter archetype, you are a nurturer and caretaker. You have a generous heart and enjoy extending your love to others. You are motivated by the most powerful of instincts – to give life and to selflessly devote yourself to the life you create. You feel compelled to care for all those around you, even if they are not your own children. In short, you feel the need to be all things to all people, and therefore your own needs sometimes go unmet. You must learn to say no, applying Artemis's sense of boundaries and Aphrodite's ability to put herself first. That way, you can give to others from an overflowing rather than a half-full cup.

The God Quiz

1. What is the most important thing in your man's life?
    a. Pursuing his dreams
    b. Being right
    c. Work
    d. Power
    e. Having a good time
    f. Analysing people
    g. Order
    h. Competition

2. How would you describe your man's temperament?
    a. Dramatic
    b. Brooding
    c. Workaholic

     d. Dominating
     e. Emotional
     f. Erratic
     g. Composed
     h. Hot-blooded

3. What about him drives you nuts when it comes to interacting as a couple?
   a. He's very clever, is hard to catch in a lie and often tricks me into letting him get his way
   b. He likes to shake things up and often introduces problems just to rattle the safety and comfort of our relationship
   c. He's not comfortable being intimate and is afraid of commitment
   d. He's charming – unfortunately, he flirts with other women!
   e. He opposes routine, has little self-control and often won't take our relationship seriously
   f. He's so mysterious I can't figure him out half the time
   g. He's so rational and in control, he likes love to be very orderly, never passionate or spontaneous
   h. He's very impulsive and restless – I'm never sure how he will react to situations or if I can count on him to stick around

4. When it comes to sex, he:
   a. Is energetic, graceful and often full of laughter
   b. Wants to try new things but, overall, is rather serious and intense
   c. Is interested in sex but is uncomfortable and lacks the skills

  d. Is an experienced, lust-filled lover – he can't get enough!

  e. Is imaginative, intuitive and inspirational

  f. Is wild, passionate and a bit of a risk taker

  g. Likes to be in control and make love routinely

  h. Is unrestrained and passionate – in fact, we have the best sex after we argue

5. On a typical Saturday afternoon, your man can often be found:

  a. Exploring something new, exciting and fun – a new restaurant, a new shop, an art gallery

  b. Hanging out at home, often alone

  c. Creating something in his workroom

  d. Volunteering for or organising a political campaign

  e. Doing something fun with his friends, especially grabbing a drink

  f. Heading to the lake with his sketchbook to draw or his laptop to do creative writing

  g. Playing tennis or golf or practising a musical instrument

  h. Playing a competitive sport like soccer, baseball, or football

6. If you were to mention that you're considering changing jobs or going back to work, your man would:

  a. Encourage you to go after your dream and not necessarily take the conventional route

  b. Encourage you to weigh the negatives against the positives

  c. Bring his job into the discussion while encouraging you to choose work that will fulfil you

    d. Discourage you – he'd rather have you stay home and take care of things than climb the corporate ladder

    e. Urge you to find an unstructured work environment – he's opposed to the nine-to-five routine and typical corporate life

    f. Make you analyse your reason for wanting to make a change and suggest that the real reason lies in your subconscious

    g. Urge you to ask yourself if you're ready for such change, especially if it will disrupt the life the two of you share

    h. Tell you to go for it, no matter what the consequences

7. When it comes to relationship arguments, your man:

    a. Is good at fixing problematic situations – he always has good solutions

    b. Isn't afraid of emotional upheavals – he thinks we can all learn a lot from difficult times

    c. Is uncomfortable arguing and not very good at making his point

    d. Is a true strategist and wins most disputes

    e. Gets very emotional and, if he feels wronged, can really fly off the handle

    f. Can get out of control and, when wronged, is extremely vengeful

    g. Likes to look at the situation calmly and rationally – he won't fight when emotions are high

    h. Is easily angered and actually enjoys a good fight

8. What profession do you think your man would be best at?
    a. Travel agent, tour guide, or public relations person
    b. Psychologist, psychiatrist, or grief counsellor
    c. Craftsman (such as a jewellery maker) or inventor
    d. Politician, business executive, school president, or headmaster
    e. Bar/club/restaurant owner or rock star
    f. Adventure guide or writer
    g. Musician, healer, or professional athlete
    h. Military man or entrepreneur

9. At a party, your man can be found:
    a. Delivering drinks and playing CDs – he's the spirit of the party
    b. Frowning in the corner, waiting to go home
    c. Engaged in conversation with a few men about work or hobbies
    d. Holding court – he loves to be centre stage
    e. Pouring drinks and making sure everyone has a great time
    f. Partying hard – he tends to get a little out of control
    g. Participating in discussion on a number of interesting topics and sharing his knowledge about them
    h. Sweating it out on the dance floor

10. Which of the following statements is most true for your man?
    a. He's filled with creativity and spontaneity – he's always up to something
    b. He keeps to himself and spends much of his time at home

c. He is most content and comfortable when he is
   working
d. He likes to be in charge and do things his way
e. He loves to party and likes to break the rules
f. He is adventurous and often urges others to take
   risks, too
g. He's knowledgeable, enjoys intellectual discussions
   and likes his world to be calm and orderly
h. He is competitive and driven to succeed

Scoring

Add up the number of a's, b's, c's, d's, e's, f's, g's and h's you
have chosen and match the answers with the gods as shown
below. A brief sketch of each god archetype follows.

Answers	Your total	Gods
A	_____	Hermes
B	_____	Hades
C	_____	Hephaestus
D	_____	Zeus
E	_____	Dionysus
F	_____	Poseidon
G	_____	Apollo
H	_____	Ares

The letter you have chosen the most represents the god who
primarily rules your man's personality. If you have chosen

the same number of two or more letters, several gods influence his personality evenly. No matter which god or gods rule his personality the most, be sure to notice the other gods, who influence him to a lesser degree, as well. Every man has aspects of all eight gods in his personality.

a. Hermes

Hermes, a son of Zeus, was the messenger of the gods. He had winged sandals and a winged hat and carried a herald's staff, or magic wand, which he used to put people to sleep and again awaken them. He led the souls of the dead to the underworld and is believed to possess magic powers over sleep and dreams. Hermes was responsible for making treaties, promoting commerce and guiding travellers. Men who embody Hermes' qualities are friendly and can bring great gain – often unexpected – to others. However, they can also be crafty and deceiving and have reputations as tricksters. Hermes men are not especially heroic or dignified, but they are clever and witty. They are full of energy and spontaneity, and delight in spurring friends out of their routines. If you are with a Hermes man, no doubt he enjoys discussing his dreams and goals and encourages you to value your own. Hermes men are constantly trying to move forward and transform – both themselves and those close to them.

b. Hades

Hades was the god of the dead, ruler of the underworld. He was also known as the lord of riches because the underworld was filled with crops and precious metals. Men ruled by Hades may be rather gloomy and unforgiving. If your man is like Hades, don't be surprised if he is not satisfied with his lot in life, as Hades was displeased when he became ruler of the underworld while his brothers, Zeus and Poseidon, controlled the sky and the sea. Typically antisocial, Hades men are more comfortable at home alone. They are familiar with dark emotions and do not shy away from them. However, they can shed light for others and help them learn from difficult experiences. A Hades man can bring enlightenment and renewal to your life. His rich inner world makes him an interesting companion.

c. Hephaestus

Hephaestus was the god of fire and metalwork and was much admired for his armour. Because he was born of Hera only, Zeus, Hera's husband, did not like him and expelled him from Mount Olympus. Eventually he returned, and Zeus apologised and gave him Aphrodite as a wife. Unlike other gods, who were all depicted as strong and attractive, Hephaestus was born lame, ugly and awkward. Men who have Hephaestus's qualities are extraordinarily creative, interested in the arts and dedicated to their work; their talents are their strong suit. They are awkward when it comes to love and it takes time for them to build intimacy. When they are devoted to a woman, they will cherish and appreciate her and be devoted to her.

d. Zeus

Zeus was the god of the sky. He was considered the protector and ruler both of the Olympian gods and of the human race. Zeus's weapon was the thunderbolt, which he threw at those who displeased him. According to legend, Zeus had two very different aspects to his personality. He was believed to be the god of justice and mercy and protector of the weak. He was also known to punish liars and breakers of oaths. Yet he himself was a philandering husband who unsuccessfully tried to keep his love affairs a secret from his irate wife, Hera. Men who embody Zeus's qualities like to be in control of their work and personal lives. Zeus men are born politicians. They are intellectual and surround themselves with people who admire and respect them. They have a great sexual appetite and are very seductive, and will do just about anything to get the girl. When they finally commit, they can be great husbands – unless, of course, they haven't overcome the Zeus weakness and need to have the occasional affair.

e. Dionysus

Dionysus was the god of wine (and cheer) and vegetation and a son of Zeus. Men ruled by Dionysus have a mysterious quality that often draws the attention – and sometimes the worship – of women. They are imaginative, intuitive and inspirational. Dionysus men are good and gentle to those who respect and pay attention to them, but to those who wrong them they are dangerous foes. They can bring madness, violence, wildness and terror. Dating a Dionysus man can be exhilarating, and don't be surprised if you find yourself letting go of your inhibitions. Be careful, though: Falling for such a man usually means falling hard, which can make the breakup (if there is one) more painful. Dionysus men have a way of making women feel more feminine, and often more emotional, too. They bring a sense of freedom that can be liberating yet also scary. For those who can handle this new-found flexibility and freedom, a relationship with a Dionysus man can be life-changing in the most positive way; for those who cannot handle this sudden departure from a routine, ordered existence, such a relationship can be disturbing, even destructive.

f. Poseidon

Poseidon was god of the sea, brother of Zeus and Hades, and second only to Zeus in power among the gods. He was married to Amphitrite but was not a faithful husband. His numerous love affairs led to the birth of children known for their wildness and cruelty. Widely worshipped by seamen, Poseidon also created the first horse. His weapon was a trident, which he would shake and use to shatter whatever he pleased. Although a Poseidon man can inspire positive change in your life, his emotional, explosive nature can sometimes lead to risky behaviour. His ability to access his emotional and artistic nature makes him a passionate lover.

g. Apollo

Apollo, a son of Zeus, was the god of prophecy, light and truth. He was a gifted musician, master archer and an accomplished athlete. Apollo's responsibilities included protecting young men, promoting agriculture and breeding of cattle, and teaching humans the arts of healing and medicine. Being that he was the god of the sun, the men under that archetype are often handsome and youthful-looking. They are characterised as self-aware, balanced, rational and eager to live a harmonious, honest life. They are noble, reasonable and organised. They go for neat, well-kept women who fit into their ordered lives. Falling in love scares Apollo men because it can be so chaotic and inexplicable, yet they do seek love and are displeased when their love is not returned. In love, they insist on controlling the relationship and can also be detached and dispassionate. If you ever break up with an Apollo man, watch out – his revenge can be harsh. As an ex-husband he will never let go.

h. Ares

Ares, the son of Zeus and Hera, was disliked by both of his parents. As the god of war, he rejoiced in battle. Ares men, too, thrive on conflict. As lovers, they may pick fights, display jealousy and act impulsively. Ares men are competitive, adventurous and live life to the fullest. Men who embody Ares qualities have a passionate instinct for life – and for love! Their unlimited energy can be used positively or negatively. While their mindless aggression can get them into criminal trouble, their assertiveness, courage and quest for achievement can lead to revolutionary advances in business, sports and elsewhere.

Chapter 3

APHRODITE,
GODDESS OF LOVE

The Aphrodite Woman: Sensuous Lover

Age cannot wither her, nor custom stale
Her infinite variety.

— WILLIAM SHAKESPEARE, *ANTONY AND CLEOPATRA*

If you are an Aphrodite woman, you are first and foremost a lover. You love having a man's attention and know how to get it. The goddess Aphrodite wore a magic girdle to attract any man she wanted; even Hera envied it and wanted to borrow it from her. Self-assured in your femininity, charismatic, passionate and uninhibited, you love pleasure and know both how to give and how to receive it. Totally comfortable in your body, you have access to the full gamut of your emotions. You feel beautiful and enjoy showing off your beauty, and you love a man who acknowledges it and tells you that you're beautiful. You live in the moment and will happily throw caution to the winds, pack a bag and go off with your lover at a moment's notice.

The golden goddess Aphrodite was born not from a conventional union but out of primal elements. As the myth goes, Uranus, god of the sky, and Gaia, goddess of the earth, were joined so closely that no light or space could separate them. To rescue his mother from this oppressive embrace, their youngest son, Cronus, ruler of time, castrated his father and threw his sex organs into the sea. Out of the salty mixture of semen and ocean water arose the primordial feminine — the beautiful, gloriously naked Aphrodite, balanced on a scallop shell.

The winds carried Aphrodite to the island of Cythera, and from there she travelled far and wide until she reached Cyprus. It was to Paphos on the island of Cyprus that she would return every spring to bathe in the sea and renew her virginity, ready for another amorous adventure.

Zeus gave Aphrodite in marriage to his son Hephaestus, the lame blacksmith of the gods, who had been cast out of Mount Olympus. The joining of such beauty with such homeliness was an odd match indeed, and Aphrodite's passionate nature led her to adulterous relations with other gods, including her husband's brother, Ares, god of war.

Together Aphrodite and Ares had four children, whom Aphrodite presented to Hephaestus as his own. Her plot worked well enough until one morning when she and Ares lingered in bed too late, and Helios, the Sun, caught them in the act. Helios hurried to inform Hephaestus, who used his smithing skills to fashion an invisible bronze net to capture the lovers during their next liaison. Hephaestus called upon the other gods and goddesses to witness the adulterers' humiliation. The goddesses, however, elected to stay home, and the gods, rather than taking Hephaestus's side, were themselves smitten by Aphrodite and wanted no part in his revenge. Hermes and Poseidon soon enough got their wish, as Aphrodite slept with each of them – before having yet another affair with Dionysus.

As her myth relates, Aphrodite is the quintessential lover, the ultimate seductress who takes endless pleasure in her own physical attributes and in bestowing her gifts upon her lovers. She resists being tamed or tied down to one man but never becomes jaded or hardened by her experiences. Rather, she remains the perpetual virgin lover, giving herself each time as if it were the first. For her, love is always the answer. As Laura Green writes in *Reinventing Home:*

> My bed is the place where it all comes together. Here is where I think naked thoughts, daydream, make love, worry, plot, argue, get my back scratched, speculate, talk about growing old and finally cut the mooring ties and drift out with the dream tide. The bed, the place where we are born and die, is our primeval place.

The goddess Aphrodite is able to enjoy her lovers without becoming attached. However, the human woman living under the Aphrodite archetype has her hands full learning to harness her sexuality and not cause herself unwanted hurt. She must develop the skill of knowing when to give herself and to whom. If she lets her sensual nature lead her, she can go with the whim of the moment, surrendering herself to a man before she knows enough about him. This is her blind spot – not seeing the whole man clearly but seeing what she wants to see, projecting onto him her archetypal longings and making him into a god. If she holds to this viewpoint, the scenario is likely to play itself out in one of two ways.

Either she eventually sees the real man with his flaws, is disappointed and lets him go, or he refuses to be the object of her projections and pushes her away. Getting caught in this trap of either fantasy or unrequited love is the Aphrodite woman's weakness. She needs to embrace the wisdom, clarity and discernment of her sister goddess Athena so she can see through the filter of her projections. She would be wise to take her man down off his pedestal, accept his vulnerabilities and allow him his imperfections – and get down off her own pedestal as well.

If a woman's sense of self-worth depends on being adored by a man, she will question her own lovability when she is on her own. For such an Aphrodite woman, an evening alone is the closest thing to hell, and a Saturday night alone is hell itself. To escape her emptiness, she may get involved in a series of affairs and lose her sense of self. She may even become obsessed with a certain man who gives her pleasure; sex with him can become a physiological addiction, very much like a drug. Her Artemis aspect can show her how to say no to sexual encounters that are not going to nurture her and help her channel her energies into creative outlets like dancing, singing, or creating fun evenings with friends.

Marilyn Monroe embodied the Aphrodite archetype in perhaps the purest form seen in recent history, and the fascination and adoration people felt and still feel for her illustrate the inexorable attraction of this unalloyed feminine archetype. However, the world so used and exploited her that she was driven into her underworld, from which she never escaped. Jane Fonda is another example of an Aphrodite woman, but she developed her Athena and Artemis aspects, and moved on from the role of Barbarella to find her voice. She became a spokesperson for women's rights by breaking away from her patriarchal relationships with her father and her husbands.

Aphrodite's unbounded freedom to love whom and when she wants makes her inherently reluctant to join with a man in the bonds of marriage. Nevertheless, at some point you may be nagged by the feeling 'I want to commit'. If you choose to pursue this wish, call on your Hera aspect to help you appreciate the comfort of love and gifts of deeper intimacy found only in a monogamous relationship. Tempering Aphrodite's loving spontaneity with Hera's resolute commitment to her spouse can make for a rich, long-lasting wedded relationship.

If the marriage loses its passion, you may become bitter and angry and start initiating affairs that eventually destroy your marriage, or you may turn to food or alcohol to deal with your emotions. Listen to that inner voice that tells you why you're unhappy. It's imperative that you identify the cycle that is stifling the passion and turn it around before you spiral down. Perhaps you are taking each other for granted. Perhaps you are dissatisfied with the way he gives you attention. Perhaps you have fallen into a routine and are not setting aside quality time for romance. Keep the channels open for communication. Get your eros evolved. Find positive ways to express your needs and help your man give you what you want. Perhaps his needs are not being met as well. On the other hand, sometimes you just need to endure the stagnation until the passion returns. If you keep investing yourself in your relationship, you might find the love that returns is of a higher soul quality.

It's not unusual for the Aphrodite woman to become a compulsive shopper and accumulate possessions – clothes, jewellery, makeup, perfumes. We often see this behaviour in famous female stars for whom it looks like nothing is ever enough. This often means that she's not receiving love and honour from herself or from her partner. More profoundly, it is a sign that the Aphrodite woman is losing the thread connecting her to her essential femininity. This compulsive accumulation of material possessions is an attempt to replace the emptiness she feels inside because she has abandoned herself and shut off her heart from herself.

An Aphrodite woman tends to succeed in any expressive art form, for instance dance, singing, acting, public relations, interior design, or clothing and jewellery design. Fields such as these offer her ample and rich opportunities for creativity and expression of her imagination. When she is emotionally connected with her work, she expresses her rich aesthetic and social gifts and can attract success and financial well-being.

As the Aphrodite woman grows older and loses her youthful sparkle, she may feel she is also losing her power. Comparing herself unfavourably to younger Aphrodites, she may choose to withdraw her energy and retreat into her shell. She should resist this tendency to contract. Like the goddess herself, the twenty-first-century Aphrodite woman must renew herself in the wellspring of her feminine power. The most important aspect of Aphrodite's myth, which is often missed, is her return home to Paphos every spring to bathe in the sea and renew herself to an even greater radiance and joy than before. These sacred baths remind us of every woman's need to dip into the source of her soul femininity, which is her hidden treasure and her birthright. It takes a willingness to go deeper into yourself, beyond the outer form. How do you do this? You can draw from your Hestia, goddess of the sacred and the centre. There is a higher form of beauty that awaits you. It is your soul eros, which is the Aphrodite woman's true power.

Aphrodite has two archetypal love matches, the brothers Hephaestus and Ares. Both are intense and highly sexual – the qualities Aphrodite most loves in a man – but one displays them outwardly as the passionate male while the other carries these qualities deep inside and funnels them into expressions of high creativity.

Her Strengths

- She is a force of nature
- She is sensual and creative
- She is assertive and knows how to put herself forward
- She loves to devote herself to her man and contribute to his happiness
- She is playful and has a great sense of fun
- Her very presence brings vitality to her relationships

Her Vulnerabilities

- She tends to lose her sense of self and look to her man to make her feel good about herself
- Her need to be in love and experience erotic pleasure can prevent her from being discerning about choosing the man who is right for her
- She tends to wear her heart on her sleeve
- She can get into serial relationships, which leave her feeling empty
- She can be too much the temptress who leaves a trail of hurt men in her wake

The Hephaestus Man: Creative Craftsman

I am a draper mad with love. I love you more than all the
flannelette and calico . . . crepon, muslin, poplin, ticking
and twill in the whole cloth of the world. I have come to
take you away to my emporium on the hill, where the change
hums on wires. Throw away your little bedsocks and Welsh
wool knitted jacket, I'll warm the sheets like an electric toaster,
I will lie by your side like the Sunday roast.

— DYLAN THOMAS, *UNDER MILK WOOD*

Hephaestus was the divine craftsman, who fabricated beautiful, magical tools and weapons for the other gods. He was
the only Greek god who worked. He was also the only god
with a deformity. The myth tells us that Hera so resented
Zeus's birthing of Athena on his own that she decided to
give birth to Hephaestus herself. But whereas Athena was
perfect, Hephaestus was born with a clubfoot. This so humiliated Hera that she rejected the child and threw him
down from Olympus. He landed on the volcanic island of
Lemnos. Two sea nymphs, Thetis and Eurynome, took him
to their home at Mukos, which in Greek means 'innermost
peace' or 'sacred place', raised him, and taught him how to
use fire. Thereafter, he used his innovative genius to create
anything that gods and mortals needed: the bed and golden
disk of the sun god, the goblets of Dionysus, the wreath
worn by Ariadne, the sickle with which Perseus beheaded
Medusa, the weapons of Hercules, the famous shield of
Achilles and ornaments for Zeus's lovers. At Zeus's command he also created Pandora, a mortal woman who had all
the charms of Aphrodite.

Hephaestus also fashioned a golden throne equipped with
invisible nets and, in a vengeful ploy, sent it to Hera as a
gift. As soon as she sat on the seat she was trapped, and no

one could set her free until Zeus promised Hephaestus Aphrodite's hand in marriage. Aphrodite, however, soon had an affair with Hephaestus's brother, Ares. When Hephaestus finally came to know of this, he captured the lovers in yet another invisible net. His fellow gods, instead of sympathising with his indignation, were themselves entranced by Aphrodite's beauty and laughed at Hephaestus for thinking he could hold such a sumptuous, magnificent goddess in a monogamous union. He suffered another humiliation when Dionysus got him drunk and brought him to Olympus on the back of a donkey.

Like the god, the Hephaestus man experiences his power through his work. It is through his work that he connects with himself and comes alive. He dives into his intense, fiery depths and produces works of beauty, grace and functionality that belie the archetype's twisted form. His sufferings and his joys alike find expression in his work, whether in the studio, at the drafting table, or in the machine shop. Or he may manifest his gifts as a chef, a gardener, a surgeon – any field that calls for work with his hands. He works not so much to earn his livelihood but because it is his passion. He has a love affair with his work; it is his true mistress. Thus it is easy for him to stay the course, devoting the long hours it takes to achieve true artistry in his field. Though he generally doesn't seek recognition, if he is blessed with real talent, success will come to him of itself. If he is not fortunate in finding work where his talents and creativity are tapped and has to take any job just to make ends meet, he risks becoming depressed and might turn to alcohol.

Having a relationship with the right woman is essential to a Hephaestus man's well-being. While his work is his passion, the woman in his life is his inspiration. She is his muse. Her beauty feeds his soul and compensates for the lack of physical grace he feels in himself, and her energy and life force draw him out of his cave. His ideal match would be an Aphrodite woman, for her radiant, exuberant femininity is a perfect counterbalance to his dense, earthbound masculinity. Once he finds his woman, he is loyal and devoted. He is so appreciative of her feminine presence in his life, she will never feel taken for granted.

The French sculptor Auguste Rodin, a Hephaestus man, had a lifetime companion and mistress, Rose Beuret, and the two of them married in what turned out to be the final year of their lives. However, during his twenties and thirties Rodin had a second lover, the young aspiring sculptor Camille Claudel, with whom he shared more interests and passions. She soon became his student, model, mistress and even collaborator. He sculpted many portraits of her and during their twenty-year relationship created many sculptures of couples in impassioned embrace, including his famous work *The Kiss*.

Since the Hephaestus man draws so much richness from within himself, he is not dependent on others to resource himself. Hephaestus's humiliation by the other gods made him a loner, and the Hephaestus man, similarly, may have few friends. He tends to be awkward in social situations and often feels like an outsider. If you happen to meet such a man at a party, he's the man who doesn't mingle and will tend to converse in monosyllables. He has a lot going on inside but just doesn't have the knack or the inclination to express it verbally. Nevertheless, though the Hephaestus man may lack in social skills, he will rely on the woman in his life to make their social plans, and he will willingly go along because it's important to her.

Like the god he lives under, the Hephaestus man may have been wounded emotionally early in life. Perhaps his mother was withdrawn and undemonstrative, and his father was critical and even abusive. Therefore he has no reference for bonding with another human, so he longs to feel a sense of belonging. And once he finds her he holds on to her and becomes dependent and needy, which might push her away. His feelings may be deeply buried, perhaps beyond his own awareness. When he is with the right woman, this fire will translate into his sexuality. He'll be a man of few words who feels his eros intensely and deeply. For him, making love can be an art form. He's totally there, focused on you, and in his hands your body becomes a sculpture that he loves every part of. And even after making love, he can hold you for hours, cherishing you.

In contrast with his brother Ares, who was quick to action and expression, Hephaestus's fire is contained, volcano-like, in the depths of him. Likewise, a Hephaestus man tends to hold his feelings deep inside. Marilyn Monroe once said about Arthur Miller, a typical Hephaestus: 'Art had such a strong face. It was a new understanding for me to see that when there was a lot of terrible tension from events, and his emotions were all in an uproar, the only way it showed was that his jaw muscles got tighter, and his skin turned yellow under the tan. . . . Art reacted a little bit like the Mafia, physically speaking.'

If he wishes to experience life more fully, the Hephaestus man needs to embrace and cultivate other aspects of himself. He needs Hermes' gift of communication and Zeus's talent for promoting himself and being more self-assertive. He would do well to awaken his Dionysus aspect – his zest for life and spontaneity, giving him permission to let go once in a while.

This is a man you might easily miss because he is not glamourous, doesn't stand out in a crowded room and doesn't boast about his achievements. But keep your eyes open for him. Look beyond the form to a man who can be solid and steady and enrich your life. He can bring you fulfilment far beyond your expectations, if you honour and accept him.

His Strengths

- He is highly creative
- He loves and appreciates the woman in his life and demonstrates it in many ways
- He can produce masterful pieces of work in the field of his choice
- He is a passionate and sensual lover
- He is aesthetically sensitive and appreciates beauty in any form

His Vulnerabilities

- He can be introverted and emotionally withdrawn
- He can feel isolated from the world
- When he has no creative outlet, he becomes enraged and depressed
- He can be volatile and explosive
- He can get so wrapped up in his work that he neglects to pay attention to his partner

The Ares Man: Impassioned Warrior

Who is the happy Warrior? Who is he
That every man in arms should wish to be?

— WILLIAM WORDSWORTH

Masculine, sensual, compulsive, ambitious, he's rough around the edges and goes for everything with passion. He's a man of action with a courageous, mighty heart and one purpose in mind – to win. His spirit is adversarial and ruthless. There is nothing proper or refined about the god of war. When the Ares man is able to positively channel his archetypal energy, he's a powerhouse. He's the football hero, ball tucked under his arm, running for the goal line; the entrepreneur closing the deal against all odds; the muscular high-rise construction worker hefting steel twenty stories up; the temperamental artist channelling his volatile nature into his performance.

When the Arian energy is not directed into constructive avenues, however, it's an archetype our society doesn't know how to handle. He's the unfathered, unloved, ignored male who goes wrong. He's the inner-city teenage boy turning to drugs. He's the man with a big goal who has no tools to cope with defeat, so if he fails, his pain leads him to self-destruct. He has a mighty heart that needs a big arena to express himself, and he needs to be educated as to how to express it.

Ares' mythology tells us a lot about his psyche. He was not wanted or cherished by anyone. His mother, Hera, conceived him by inadvertently touching an herb that could make any woman fertile. His father, Zeus, disparaged him for his quarrelsome nature. Even the Greeks themselves did not honour this god with his own temple. As a child, he was captured by twin giants, the Aloadae, who shut him in a bronze jar, where he remained for thirteen months until he was rescued by Hermes. Maybe it was while locked in the jar that he built the persona of a warrior, vowing that such a thing would never happen to him again. This image of Ares bottled up gives us an insight into the Ares psyche, how the man feels inside himself. Ares' tutor, Priapus, taught him to dance and thus find a creative channel for his formidable energies. So also, it is imperative for the Ares man to express his pent-up energy through sports or other intense physical activities. You will recognise him in tennis player John McEnroe, who had regular tantrums on the court.

In Shakespeare's *Othello* we see an Ares character in action. He doesn't trust his heart. And his rage and his inability to discern clearly let him believe the lies that Iago feeds him, and he ends up destroying the woman he most loves.

Ares is famous for his impassioned relationship with Aphrodite. However, he and his half sister Athena were perpetually in conflict. She is a peaceful warrior who goes into battle using strategy and with a clear purpose: to protect. Ares, on the other hand, loves war's chaos and bloodshed. She avoids conflict, while he thrives on it. In Homer's *Iliad* she calls him a bully, wounds him on the battlefield and at another point strips him of his weapons to stop him from fighting.

Think of Tom Jones as the quintessential Ares man – earthy and physical, with a giant sexual appetite. What you, as an Aphrodite woman, relish about him is his total participation in life, whether he's eating, drinking, dancing, working, participating in sports, or – of course – making love. Professional athletes are often Ares personalities, and more often than not, they're married to an Aphrodite woman. These guys just love to bring home the trophy and ravish you in bed, and you, in turn, will do everything you can to make them feel like winners.

If you are dating or married to an Ares man, you might find that he lacks sensitivity to your feelings and can be completely blind to your point of view. Yet his rough masculinity arouses your femininity. He needs to be with a woman who does not reject his masculine sensuality in any way and does not live in her head. His sexuality is raw, unabashed and exuberant. That pent-up energy has an enormous appetite for the female body. He can make love to you for hours and relish every part of your body and return for more. If you're on a first date with an Ares man and there's physical attraction between you, it will be very hard to resist surrendering to him before the evening is over.

He's not a big conversationalist. You won't find him philosophising about life or analysing his feelings. He finds other ways to bond with his male friends – over drinking and talking about sports or women, and his language can be crude. He makes decisions quickly. There's nothing diplomatic about him. He calls it as he sees it, thereby often alienating colleagues and friends. He likes to feel in control all the time. That's how he experiences his power. If he feels he is losing control, he may try to manipulate the situation to regain his sense of authority. As his partner, you may be the one who helps him polish his rough edges, pointing out his blind spots and suggesting alternative behaviours. He can be myopic about other people and how he interacts with them, and it can cost him in his personal life and his work. You may find yourself helping him open his eyes.

In his negative aspect, the Ares man can be quick to anger, abusive and irrational. This behaviour has its roots in a wounded psyche. If as a child he was not cherished and loved for who he is but was instead suppressed, humiliated and punished, he will try to compensate by always fighting to win. He might lock horns with other Ares men, or become a rebel. There is a scene in D. H. Lawrence's novel *Women in Love*, where the friends Rupert and Gerald wrestle naked beside a roaring fire in the drawing room; this is a quintessential Ares scene. The plethora of heavy testosterone movies where the characters defy authority and blow things up, like the *Terminator* series, *The Rock* and *Con Air*, are nothing more than society's attempt to work out its relationship with the Ares archetype.

Marriage to an Ares man can become challenging if he is frustrated at work and can't find enough outlets for his energy. If he brings the frustration home and his wife starts putting pressure on him, he might go to battle with her. You have to be very smart with your Ares man. You should encourage him to find activities that will consume his intense, passionate energy. A friend of mine who is married to an Ares man helped him find an opportunity to coach a high school soccer team. Not only was it a physical outlet for him, but as a mentor he could use his enthusiasm and gusto to inspire the teenagers and give them direction. A great coach, he was loved and recognised for his gifts.

Underneath the Ares man's aggressive exterior is an insecure and self-doubting ego. And underneath that is a passionate heart that is looking for a safe way to express itself. If his Aphrodite woman is strong and secure in herself, she can remove his armour without leaving him feeling threatened or exposed. Then his huge masculine heart will open to love and he will feel his true power, which does not require him to conquer anything.

In the myth, the one who releases Ares from his imprisonment is the mercurial messenger of the gods, Hermes. Likewise, embracing his Hermes archetype may help the Ares man find ways to lighten up his load. Hermes can teach him fluidity and to be more playful, to relax and have fun. As an

Ares man finds resolution for his bottled-up emotions and learns to channel his energies creatively, he gains command over himself. Once tamed, his intense energy can be attractive to others. He may become a gifted leader and great at mobilising people to achieve their goals. When the Ares man lines up with his giant spirit and directs his energy toward you, surrounding you with it, you feel enlivened and enriched, and the woman in you will feel fully acknowledged.

His Strengths

- He is courageous and a risk taker
- He loves and thrives on a woman's femininity
- He is a passionate, sensual lover
- He perseveres until his goal is reached and is inventive in overcoming obstacles
- He can be a reliable, protective family man
- He is a leader and mobiliser of others

His Vulnerabilities

- He can be impulsive and react quickly without thinking of the consequences
- If he is challenged he may be quick to strike out
- He can be insensitive and even abusive
- He can be self-centred and blind to the woman's point of view
- He can be territorial and possessive, leading to irrational jealousy concerning his partner
- He can mistrust others and think everyone is against him

Aphrodite and Hephaestus: Work and

Music I heard with you was more than music,
And bread I broke with you was more than bread.

— CONRAD AIKEN

When a Hephaestus man first meets and falls in love with his Aphrodite, it's as if he has discovered the divine. The world takes on a new light for him, and he glimpses for the first time the expression of love. Marilyn Monroe described Arthur Miller's first impression of her: 'I happened to see Arthur's notebook. He had left it lying wide open for me to see. On the first page he'd written that in the beginning I almost made him believe in God, I had been so beautiful and angelic.'

Your Hephaestus man will see you as his personal goddess. Feeling protected and safe in his presence, you will blossom, get in touch with your beauty and truly feel like a goddess yourself. Although the attraction between you may not be obvious to others, the chemistry can be fiery and passionate. Making love to you is an experience he feels intensely inside; however, he might not verbalise what he's feeling. You, on the other hand, who love to know how much you are appreciated, might wish to hear more from him. Just go with him, and tune in to his communication, which is happening on other levels.

One of the ways he shows how much he appreciates having you in his life is his generosity. Hephaestus men can shower you with gifts, flowers, and if they have the means, their credit cards, too. He can be highly creative in the way he pleases you. You might admire a painting at a friend's house, and a few days later find that he has gone to the trouble to purchase the same for you and hang it on your wall. He might surprise you with an unexpected trip. It makes him happy to know that he's contributing to your well-being and happiness. And one of the greatest compliments you can pay him is to let him know you are so happy to be with him – not just that you love him but that you enjoy being in his presence. Remember, in the Hephaestus myth none of the other gods were happy to have him in their presence, though they were pleased with what he produced for them. In his relationship with you, the Hephaestus man can learn that he is loved for who he is as much as for what he does.

What attracts a Hephaestus man to you is your openness and vitality. If sometimes at the beginning of your relationship he appears to be insecure and withdrawn, do not take it personally and pull back. It's in his nature to be critical of himself and afraid of making the wrong move. Keep being your wonderful self and, regardless of his behaviour in the moment, let your expressiveness draw him out.

When he gives himself over to his work, the woman in his life becomes his muse. She may also take care of his basic needs, organise his social life and shape the way he presents himself to the world. He is monogamous and will expect you to be as well, but if he makes the fatal mistake of withdrawing his attention from you in favour of his work, you may well seek passion elsewhere. That is why it is essential that you keep communicating to him your needs and your wants. Your love for him will find ways to draw him out so you won't need to look for affection outside your relationship.

One of the challenges this relationship can face is if he is stuck in a job that doesn't allow him creative expression, or if he loses his job or retires and doesn't have an expressive outlet. It may seem as though the fire has gone out. His passion won't be there to enliven you, so you can become unhappy and even lose your respect for him. Moreover, because he has nowhere to put his creativity, he can become angry or depressed. This can be a significant time of transition for him. All his life he has identified himself with his work. Now it seems as if his soul has designed an opportunity for him to touch into who he is rather than what he does.

At such a time, the Aphrodite woman can be strategic in helping her Hephaestus man come out of this stuck place. When he is circumscribed and withdrawn, she can continue to be his muse, helping him to find outlets. Because he responds to beauty and functionality, keep putting beauty before him. Invite him to visit an art museum or perhaps an auto show or a boat show. Choose a movie that you think will engage him and help him release some of that buried energy.

There are times in the Hephaestus/Aphrodite relationship when the woman might seek ways that would assist her to grow. She might attend seminars, retreats, classes that help her develop deeper parts of herself. You may want him to come along with you and open up more, but he cannot, or will not. It's best to leave him alone in this regard and enjoy the aspects of him that are available to you. Love him for what he shows you, and leave the rest to unfold according to its own timing. Always include him in your experiences by sharing your exuberance with him. This is what nourishes and sustains him.

Aphrodite and Ares: Turbulent Passion

Eternity was in our lips and eyes,
Bliss in our brows' bent; none our parts so poor,
But was a race of heaven.

– WILLIAM SHAKESPEARE,
ANTONY AND CLEOPATRA 1.3.35–37

Ares and Aphrodite are the archetypal lovers. The polar opposite of his creative and contained brother Hephaestus, Ares is the quintessential conqueror – and Aphrodite loves to be conquered. The union between an Aphrodite woman and an Ares man is the most physical, erotic and intense of all relationships. She softens his rough edges; he grounds her fluid female energy. When their energies match, they can come together in the ideal alchemical union of the pure female and the pure male. Painters, poets and authors have exalted this union – they have just never told us how to make it happen day to day!

I can think of no one who has better described the fusion of an Ares man and an Aphrodite woman than D. H. Lawrence:

> His arms were fast around her, he seemed to be gathering her into himself, her warmth, her softness, her adorable weight, drinking in the suffusion of her physical being, avidly. He lifted her, and seemed to pour her into himself like wine into a cup. . . .
>
> So she relaxed, and seemed to melt, to flow into him, as if she were some infinitely and precious suffusion filling into his veins, like an intoxicant. Her arms were around his neck, he kissed her and held her perfectly suspended, she was all slack and flowing into

him and he was the firm, strong cup that receives the wine of her life. So she lay cast upon him, stranded, lifted up against him, melting and melting under his kisses, melting into his limbs and bones, as if he were soft iron becoming surcharged with her electric life.

Till she seemed to swoon, gradually her mind went, and she passed away. Everything in her was melted down and fluid, and she lay still, became contained by him, sleeping in him as lightning sleeps in a pure, soft stone. So she was passed away and gone in him, and he was perfected.

In the mythology, the union of Aphrodite and Ares produced four children: the sons Deimos (Fear) and Phobos (Panic), the daughter Harmonia (Harmony) and another son, Eros. Thus the ancient psychology lets us know that this ideal relationship can produce two states of being: love and balance, or fear and terror. To grasp the Aphrodite and Ares relationship, think, for instance, of the intense attraction yet volatility of Elizabeth Taylor and Richard Burton, or Stanley and Stella in *A Streetcar Named Desire*.

Although the Ares man isn't likely to initiate marriage plans, he's likely to agree to marriage if that's what you want. And, once married, he'll be a stable and reliable family man so long as you don't deprive him of activities with his male companions, such as playing cards, engaging in sports, or going out for a few beers. He needs these outlets to release his pent-up energy, and if he doesn't have them, he's more likely to become aggressive toward you, perhaps becoming abusive or turning to alcohol as his outlet.

If he does begin to make home his personal battlefield, don't fall into the trap of becoming his adversary. If he becomes like a wild horse, draw upon your brilliant strategist,

Athena, be strong, and hold on to the reins. Don't let him run rampant, for he will take you with him. Avoid challenging him, judging him, rejecting him, or trying to change him. Turn your passion into compassion; keep loving him past his behaviour. Call on the clarity and wisdom of Athena. Learn to access the power of your intuition, which will reveal to you what is needed in the moment. If you know how to step back from his intensity and not judge how he is expressing it, creative solutions will come to you in the moment. You can discern when to hold your peace, when to say just a few words, when to go to bed with him and when to simply get out of the house! Especially in an Ares/Aphrodite relationship, action is more powerful than a thousand words. You also need Artemis's keen sense of boundaries to let him know that unleashed anger isn't allowed. If he's in a state, you get out of there. Try to leave the drama of *Who's Afraid of Virginia Woolf?* for the movies.

Because of your emotional nature, as an Aphrodite woman, you could be victimised by the Ares whirlwinds and start to lose your sense of self. Listen to your Hestia. It is essential that you keep returning to yourself as the source of your own well-being. (This is not the moment to turn to him to feel good about yourself.) He will then respect you and realise that he has to do things differently if he doesn't want to lose you.

When the relationship is in a positive upswing, you feel protected by him, and that provides you with a foundation to be even freer and enhance your gifts, enjoy the zest for life and be involved in the things that give you pleasure and make you truly happy.

Margaret's Story: Aphrodite Discovered

Margaret is a beautiful, fifty-one-year-old woman who came of age as a flower child in the sixties. She still sees the world through the lens of an uncorrupted, free spirit, despite all she has experienced. When still young, she met and married a workaholic businessman with whom she had two children. He provided generously for her and the children but paid them little attention, devoting all his time and energy to his work. Despite two lovely children and a beautiful home in a Connecticut suburb, there was no marriage to speak of – and certainly no passion.

She lived this way for twenty-five years until she met a Hermes-like man with whom she fell in love. Although they had no sexual relations, the attraction was strong enough to awaken her Aphrodite and make her realise she'd been too long in the underworld and needed to reemerge into the light. She asked for a divorce, got a generous settlement and bought land on which to build a house of her own in a nearby town.

Wanting to spend some time alone sorting out her thoughts, she decided to rent a cottage at the beach for a week. To her surprise, on the second day she met and fell in love with Scott, a carpenter. Her newly awakened Aphrodite had attracted a Hephaestus man, a craftsman, who adored and made passionate love to her. Their affair continued for a year – she would spend at least one weekend a month at the beach – until construction of her house began.

That's when she met Matt, a construction contractor. Matt was a good-looking, outgoing man – again so different from what she had known – and Margaret fell madly in love with him. The attraction was mutual, but there was a problem – Matt was happily married with three children and was not about to leave his family. They resisted for a while but ultimately gave in and began a sexual relationship, making love early in the morning, during breaks in his workday and after the other workers had gone home – before he went home to his wife and kids. Both of them were consumed with guilt yet unable to let go of each other. Margaret even began to fantasise that his wife would die and he would be free, but then she felt even guiltier about having such thoughts. In the meantime, Scott kept calling, wanting to meet up with her, and she always made up a story why she couldn't go – the truth being she was all tied up with Matt.

Margaret and I sat in her garden one afternoon drinking tea, and she confided her dilemma to me. She had stayed in a loveless marriage because of her children. Now she was free and her Aphrodite energies were awake, and she'd become involved with a married man with whom there was no hope of a long-term relationship. This was a woman capable of love and loyalty who was still in the process of maturing and finding her authentic self.

She had to make some choices. As her house reached completion she would no longer be in daily contact with Matt, and not seeing him regularly would make it easier to separate from him. She decided to treat the process of disconnecting like weaning a baby from the breast. She would talk with Matt on the phone and share her feelings with him but not invite him to the house. She made a decision to observe herself as she went through this change, and use her mind to disengage from her emotions. She would enlist the support of the few friends who knew about the situation. She also decided to go back to the beach house where she felt nurtured and spend more time with herself, walking on the beach, writing and meditating, and occasionally seeing Scott just as a friend.

Coming out of a passionate entanglement that doesn't work requires you to have tough love for yourself, which calls for gentleness and patience, and at the same time firmness and ruthlessness. This is where Athena has to become your ally. Margaret was definitely moving in the right direction by focusing her attention toward a man who *is* available.

Opening up to Aphrodite's passion after it's been locked away for a long time is a most enlivening experience. However, be sure to choose wisely.

Elaine and Mike:
Opening the Channels of Communication

An Aphrodite friend of mine, Elaine, was married to Mike, an Ares man, and within a year of their marriage they had a child. Soon after the child was born, Mike started going out drinking with 'the guys' occasionally after work. As these evenings became longer and more frequent, Elaine began to wonder if he was having an affair. Her suspicions and resentment grew; she began to question him when he got home, and then to doubt his answers, and invariably her questioning would lead to an argument.

She called me one night, desperate – ready to walk out on him, or kill him, or at least hurt him in some way. She did leave him that night, saying she was going to stay with friends, and the next day she sought counselling. With the help of the therapist, Elaine made two decisions: She would continue her therapy and she would stop blaming Mike for her feelings.

When things at home become tense and argumentative, it's the Athena ingenuity that prompts you to take time-out *before* things get worse. Sometimes simply walking around the block a couple of times is enough to break the negative cycle. Whatever you do, don't just stand there in the middle of the minefield!

Elaine came to realise that she resented Mike's having made her pregnant before they had had time to enjoy their romance. She was now a wife and a mother and, worst of all, a housekeeper – a deadly job for any Aphrodite woman. She felt trapped and enraged. Mike had sensed her hostile emotions and couldn't wait to get out of the house. The angrier she became, the more he needed to escape; the more time he spent with his friends, the angrier she became – a true vicious circle.

Opening up to the nurturing and mothering qualities of her Demeter and the gifts of her inner Hera, Elaine was able to surrender better to her role as a mother and a wife and be grateful for her beautiful family. She felt empowered and then could appreciate what Mike had been feeling, and stopped blaming him for her unhappiness.

Together, Elaine and Mike were able to set up some new parameters for their relationship. One night a week she would go out with her girlfriends and have some fun on her own. He would agree to be home at a certain time, and he'd call if he were going to be late. Twice a month they'd arrange an evening for themselves and have a 'date'. And they agreed they would never again go to bed angry.

Mike began to romance Elaine all over again, bringing her flowers and calling during the day to remind her that he loved her. Elaine treated herself to little things that made her feel better about herself – new lingerie, a manicure, a pedicure, a facial. She continued her counselling so she would be sure to keep up with her side of the agreement. And Mike, as a result of her new attitude, gained confidence in himself and began to get involved in sports.

Who says that if you marry you must stop being the glorious Aphrodite? Who says that if you have children you can no longer be joyful and fun loving? You can be a mother to a child and still be a sensual, beautiful woman. If you join with your goddess sisters – Hera, Demeter and Athena – instead of cutting yourself off from the powers they offer you, you can embrace the loving happiness that surely awaits you.

Aphrodite Speaks

So tell me about your beauty, your irresistible attraction.

All women are born beautiful.
Knowing that, however, is their choice!
All women are born deserving love.
Choosing that is up to them.
I have no bonds or boundaries;
I love whom I choose and when I want.
I'm free in my love; I am in bliss.
In my senses I rejoice.
You do not choose me –
You're afraid of my freedom –
You judge me.
You pollute me with your thoughts, your shame and
    your guilt.
I'm moved to ecstasy when I love;
When I mate I become one.
I know how.
Everything that breathes and is alive comes under my
    domain:
Doves, dolphins, swans,

Roses, irises, lilies.
All pleasures and sensuous delights,
Perfumes and oils,
Lustrous fabrics, food and drink.
Music thrills my soul:
The lyre, the harp, those soft sounds make love
   to me.
The waves of the sea –
Oh, yes, there you'll see me,
In the ocean,
In the sunsets,
All the exquisite beauty between birth and death,
When day meets the night.
Why do you fear death?
I die every time I mate. I am in ecstasy.
I give myself over and over and over again
To the glory that is love in the moment.
I have no fear of losing myself.
Oh, there is the secret:
To give oneself and keep oneself intact.
That is my bliss, my mortal, divine bliss.
I know who I am.
I smile. Can you see
My secret smile?
To whom do I belong?
I belong to me.

Chapter 4

HESTIA, GODDESS OF THE HEARTH AND HOME

The Hestia Woman: A Soulful Presence

A billion stars go spinning through the night,
Blazing high above your head.
But in you is the presence that will be,
When the stars are dead.

— RAINER MARIA RILKE

Always connected to her spiritual compass, the Hestia woman is content within herself and with being of service to life. She doesn't seek attention. She moves in the world yet is not of the world because she is not ambitious and has no agenda to achieve or succeed. She is about being. Her home is her sanctuary, and she infuses it with soul that permeates every corner. Glamour eludes her and fashion is not even on her radar screen, yet she is majestic and elegant in spirit.

To others she might look passive, lacking expression, but her gift is more subtle – a capacity to see the glorious simplicity of each moment and silently marvel at the miracle of life. Her clarity allows her to receive guidance from within. She is like those clear days after a rain when everything is crisp and moist, pure and renewed. Graceful, with an air of civility, she extends respect to everyone. You might pass her by without even noticing her. But lucky is the man who chooses to give her the golden apple and make her his own. She will illuminate his world and bring a depth that will enrich his life. In the myth of Paris choosing the fairest of the goddesses, the contestants were Aphrodite, Athena and Hera. Hestia was not even in the competition. He gave the golden apple to Aphrodite, and that is how the ten-year Trojan War started – a telling account of how men's seeking after obvious beauty and sexuality has often led to a downfall.

According to Plato, the name 'Hestia' means the essence of things. She is the most anonymous, the least personal of all the goddesses. There were no temples built for her, or statues carved. Yet Hesiod called her the chief of the goddesses. As eldest daughter of the Titans Rhea and Cronus, she is the oldest goddess in the Greek pantheon and sister of Zeus and Poseidon. All the gods, even Zeus, showed her respect. As the goddess of the hearth, she protected the fire that burned at the centre of every ancient Greek home and in the public hearth of every city. Her perpetual flame is the source to which life returns to be replenished. Like Athena and Artemis, she is a virgin goddess, never entering into union with a male. Like the flame she guards, she remains pure and undefiled.

Hestia's life energy burns for the family, for society and, most of all, for individual souls. The Hestia woman is a healer. She listens with her soul, and her very listening is a balm, providing comfort and release. She doesn't have a single vein of narcissism and she cares unconditionally for others, whom she sees as sacred. She is accepting and non-judgmental. Hestia women teach us how to protect our souls from the world's triviality and chaos.

A dear Hestia friend of mine is a gifted massage therapist. As I lie on her massage table I dive deeper into myself, and she can tell within minutes what has been going on with me because she is so attuned. My body releases the frenzy of the world, my mind settles and I slide into the centre of my heart. As the session ends, I feel as if I have been nourished with the food of the gods. Hestia women make wonderful therapists, as they are compassionate and patient. Or they may choose to be nurses or work in nonprofit organisations. Or they might take part in relief programmes, caring for those in need.

The Hestia woman's home is decorated simply but beautifully. The whole environment exudes a sense of harmony and peace. Her closet is filled with comfortable clothes – practical and flowing, nothing too fitted and most likely lots of flat shoes. She probably wears little makeup, and when she finds clothing she loves, she tends to keep wearing that style for years. She dresses for comfort, not for attention.

In the movie *Mr. T. and the Women*, Farrah Fawcett plays a woman who suffers from a nervous breakdown. The psychiatrist, played by Lee Grant, calls her condition a Hestia complex and explains to her puzzled husband, played by Richard Gere, that it is the need of a woman to break from materiality and return to her sacred, childlike self.

In her relationships with men, the Hestia woman definitely waits for the man to make the move. She is patient, like Eleanor Dashwood in *Sense and Sensibility*, who knows how to endure and wait for romance to come. And aren't we all relieved when Edward Ferrars finally comes to his senses and confesses his love for her! A Hestia woman can easily remain disconnected from her body and her emotional nature, so she may miss the fact that she is attracted to a man unless he keeps coming around. Once she feels her erotic self connecting with her heart, she can fall in love.

Unlike Aphrodite, who can lose track of her inner listener when she is attracted to a man, Hestia is much more centred. Therefore it is harder for her to be swayed and lose her clarity of vision. The Hestia woman has the ability to contain herself even in the midst of attraction, thus she does not appear needy. On the other hand, by holding herself back she risks missing the whole dance – and there is the possibility that she doesn't want to dance.

If you are a Hestia woman, you need a man who is connected to spirit and appreciates your depth, who can make love to you in a most sensual and affectionate way. As long as he knows how to draw you out from your hearth but not invade you, you will be fulfiled being with him. You will be enriched by the expansion that comes with the relationship, even though it means moving out of your comfort zone.

If you are interested in joining the dance, remember that you have the power to attract the relationship to yourself. And who knows better than you how to ask from your source for something and draw it to you? Why not give love a chance? Set an intention for life to bring you your Hermes. And take the necessary actions to implement the intention – make yourself more available, strike up conversations with single men, dress differently, decide to date. Choose yourself. Give yourself the golden apple. As you open to love in a personal way, you can give breath to your intimate, feminine aspects. As you experience the joys and challenges of a personal relationship, you will experience the power of the two merging as one.

Her Strengths

- She knows how to transform the mundane into the sacred
- She is gifted at turning a house into a home
- She brings her steadiness and her loyalty to her relationships
- Her soulfulness is her magnetism
- She is centred and a great listener
- She is full within herself

Her Vulnerabilities

- She can become so absorbed in her spirituality that she is cut off from her sensuality
- She can be complacent about lovemaking
- She can ignore signs that her partner needs more attention
- She can become too placid and serious and not have fun
- She can deny her own needs
- She can be too much of a homebody and not want to go out much

The Hermes Man: Enchanting Wanderer

He charms the eyes of men or awakens whom he wills.

– HOMER, *THE ODYSSEY*

I remember as a young girl seeing the statue of Hermes at Olympia, Greece, for the first time. I was transfixed by the soul of beauty and mystery that the sculptor Praxiteles had breathed into the marble. Even in stone, Hermes (also known by his Roman name, Mercury) has the power to charm. There was Hermes the alchemist with his curly hair, carrying his baby brother, Dionysus, to the nymphs. His magnetic smile conveys the mystical connection we all long for, and the gaze of affection in his eyes touches the viewer's soul. The statue captures the powerful symbol of Hermes holding the primordial divine child – the child within each of us that, if we are lucky, we never outgrow.

Born in Arcadia in a cave on Mt. Cyllene, out of the union of Zeus and Maia, Hermes participated in his first act of insolence while still an infant. On the day of his birth, the audacious child crawled away from Maia's cave and entered the world on his own. He then proceeded to make his first mark in the Olympic pantheon as the god of transformation.

The first creature he encountered outside the cave was a slow-moving tortoise. He killed it, gutted it and covered its shell with ox leather. Out of pure ingenuity he then made strings from the intestines of a lamb and attached them to the shell, transforming these raw materials and inventing the lyre. He proceeded to sing and play on his new instrument, making music that evoked joy, love and sweet sleep.

Later that same day, when most newborn infants would be happy with mother's milk, Hermes decided he was hungry for meat. He precociously ventured forth from the cave again and stole fifty of his half brother Apollo's cows. He skinned and barbecued two of the cows, made an offering to the gods and ate the remainder. With full stomach, he returned to the cave and fell asleep on his cot, his lyre tucked neatly under his arm.

Apollo was furious with Hermes and demanded that his

cattle be returned. Hermes pleaded innocent, claiming that he was merely an infant and could not have taken them. Apollo brought him in front of Zeus and demanded that Hermes confess his act to their mighty father. Hermes again denied he had anything to do with stealing Apollo's cows. Zeus, though amused by his young son's mastery of lying, ordered Hermes to show his brother where he had hidden the cattle and return them.

The two brothers eventually reconciled, and a bond was established between them through an exchange of gifts. Hermes gave Apollo the lyre. Apollo promised to love Hermes more than any of Zeus's other children and gave him the fifty cows plus a gold staff that would become his symbol.

With his rod in his hand, his winged sandals on his feet, and his petasus (the hat worn by travellers) on his head, Hermes travels faster than the wind and is protector of travellers, athletes, businessmen and thieves. In the lead role of the movie *Chariots of Fire,* the Scottish runner Eric Liddell, at the height of running the Olympic 400-metre race, asks himself, 'Where does the power come from to win the race?' The answer flashes in his mind: 'From within'. This is the source that Hermes knows how to tap. As messenger of the gods he travels with ease between worlds – from Olympus to earth or the underworld. Because of his role as communicator between the worlds, he is also protector and guide of souls as they traverse the underworld. Hermes, the god of the wind, thus becomes the god of the dead because the human soul is like a breath of wind when it leaves the body.

Hermes is the patron of orators, philosophers and writers because of his eloquent persuasiveness. It was he who invented the alphabet and numbers. When Zeus wanted to free his beloved Io from Argus, the hundred-eyed monster, he appealed to Hermes. Hermes disguised himself as a shepherd, and as he began to speak and play his shepherd's pipe, his words caressed Argus's ears until the monster couldn't keep his eyes open, and so Zeus was able to reclaim her.

Hermes is unabashed about all aspects of himself, including his sexuality. His most famous son, Hermaphroditus, shares Hermes' name as well as his androgynous and bisexual nature, along with the name and sexual idiosyncrasies of his mother, Aphrodite. Hermes' passionate nature leads him to pursue nymphs and maidens, who often run to escape his charms. He has the ability to infuse that passion into all who follow and embrace him. As much as he loves to chase, however, Hermes never allows himself to be caught. Ever elusive and on the move, he is the one god without a long-term love interest. Hermes will do anything to achieve a goal and is skilful at devising ways to follow his many whims – with no shame or remorse. He is infamous as the trickster, the charming deceiver. He has no qualms about lying.

Many Hermes men are successful at what they do without having completed a formal education. Beatrix Potter's comment, 'Thank goodness I was never sent to school; it would have rubbed off some of the originality' could very well apply to the Hermes man. Charming, intelligent, persuasive, always on the move – he is an original. He is Leonardo DiCaprio in the film *Catch Me If You Can,* changing into different personalities while still charming us. He is Nick Nolte in *Down and Out in Beverly Hills* making connections with everyone in the family, even the dog. A songwriter friend of mine who is the quintessential Hermes spirit once described to me how he managed to get into a completely sold out Wimbledon tennis tournament. Not only did he get in free, but he sat in the front row next to one of the players. When the ticket collector came to check the seats, my friend turned to the tennis player and said, 'I don't have a ticket.' She took his hand and said, 'Don't worry. You are with me.'

Ah, the Hermes charm! Warren Beatty and Hugh Grant are perfect examples of Hermes men. Both possess enough charm to seduce countless women around the world, in the movies and in real life! Like bees that travel from flower to flower, Hermes men often act like Don Juan going from woman to woman until they find the woman who centres them and pulls them home.

How does Hermes get away with such outrageous trickery and deception? Because it serves a purpose. He shakes us out of our rational plans and frees us from our need to control. Like Apollo, we are perhaps angry at first with Hermes' trickery, but ultimately we fall a happy casualty to his charming lack of guile. His spirit is fluid, trusting, open to signs and coincidences, and comfortable with the unforeseeable and unexpected. He reminds us of the childlike, divine innocence in us all, our closest connection to the origin of our spirit.

His Strengths

- He is adventurous, spontaneous and fun to be with
- He has a quick and agile mind and is a brilliant communicator
- His charm draws people who are ready to help him achieve his goals
- He can help us all find delight in the unexpected
- He is gifted in making connections for himself and others
- He always finds a way out of a fix

His Vulnerabilities

- He is unreliable
- He can make you fall for him completely – and then disappear
- He can be an opportunist, drawing from you what he needs in the moment
- He can be manipulative and impulsive
- Even in marriage he likes to maintain a certain independence
- He can feel entitled to the world treating him a certain way

Hestia and Hermes:
Keeping the Hearth Ablaze

Sensual pleasure passes and vanishes in the twinkling of an eye,
but the friendship between us, the mutual confidence,
the delights of the heart, the enchantment of the soul,
these things do not perish and can never be destroyed.
I shall love you until I die.

– VOLTAIRE

As a Hestia woman, goddess of the hearth, you understand the value of sacred space whether that be your home or your spiritual centre. You know your life's meaning springs from your inner self. So you may be quite content being on your own, not seeking a relationship. When a Hermes man enters your world, he opens your mind to new vistas. He loves adventure and will take you with him. If you fall in love with him, your heart will open like the morning light on a spring day. He will call forth your fullness and your brightness. If your heart has been a calm, clear lake, reflecting everything around it, in Hermes' presence you will discover its depths and its currents. The to-do list goes out the window, the chores of life take a backseat for a while, and you and this magical man connect deeply.

Our binding female nature that wants security and commitment may want to stay connected forever. But Hermes would respond, 'What is forever?' For he lives in the moment. Your Hermes man will not be confined or defined. From the moment he was born, Hermes always did what he wanted. His first act of defiance, stealing his brother's cows and lying about it, tells us he is an independent thinker who lives by his own rules. Childlike, he is not malicious. He just loves to break conventions and does not like to be confined by the ordinary.

He follows the wind beneath his wings wherever it might take him. You might be tempted to lose your centre and chase after him, to make him *the one*. But if you try to cling and analyse his ways, he will resist, put on his winged sandals and fly away. This is the time to amplify your Hestia centredness so you are conscious of your emotions toward this man. You'll want your Athena wisdom to counsel you. You'll need her clear-sightedness so you do not run away with your fantasies – or let him run away with them. Hermes men don't get trapped in their fantasies. They can rapidly detach themselves.

If your feminine psyche has been starved, if your Aphrodite has stayed protected for a long time, if you yearn to be stirred up, Hermes might show up in your life. Even unconsciously we may long for the mystical, magical part of us that wants to be more alive, that wants to break through the mundane; and thus, unknown to ourselves, we may be calling him. This happened to me when I fell in love with a

Hermes man. Little did I know that I had drawn him to me to release me from my self-confinement, to teach me how to play and discover more of my soulful feminine self. He extracted from life what was delightful, fun and adventurous, and if there was none he would create it. He always brought me out of my seriousness and made me laugh. I look at pictures of myself with him and see joy spilling out of my skin. I fell in love with him, but in fact it was me I was falling in love with. My eros was awakened and provided glimpses into my soul. Naturally, I associated all those elements with him and wanted to cling. But my fear of losing him was in fact fear of losing a newly discovered me.

Hermes is known throughout history as an alchemist who transforms base metals into gold. He comes to help us transmute our baser self into our divine self. If you are willing to unravel the strings of control and let go of all expectations and demands, you'll become softer, more accepting, and allow your own self to be set free. The best approach with the Hermes man, though it's also the most challenging, is being comfortable with the unknown. Enjoy his adventurous qualities and partake in his way of doing life, so different from your own. Can you enjoy him and not give your power to him? If you can, you're in for an amazing, delightful surprise.

The challenge for any Hestia and Hermes pair is to continue to inspire each other. Hermes can teach Hestia to find the extraordinary in the ordinary, to embrace the element of unexpectedness. Tapping into your childlike spontaneity and wonder will bring the relationship happiness. And how can Hestia inspire Hermes? When Hermes falls in love with Hestia, he feels he has come home. Her soulfulness and depth soothe him. Perhaps he calls her from a business meeting that has gone awry and she calms his discontent.

She knows how to build boundaries to protect their home from the invasions of the outside world; she protects the soul of their relationship, making sure the world's chaos doesn't go to bed with them. She is his harbour. She has the capacity to receive him unconditionally. She is accepting and nonjudgmental, and though she sees his rough edges, she doesn't resist them. The true beauty of why this relationship works is because he doesn't feel trapped. He, in turn, becomes the catalyst for the Hestia woman to connect her spirit with her body. He is her anchor. That is the great gift he brings her. Then her soul, heart and body become a temple. Therefore, the more conscious they are of that energy in their lovemaking, the richer and more sacred it is. He makes love not just to her body but to her soul.

The backbone of the Hermes and Hestia relationship is the freedom they can create between them. They're secure in their connection. She can move on with her day and keep the fire burning at home while he is out creating adventures or pursuing entrepreneurial deals. She doesn't obsess: 'Oh, I wonder what he is doing now. He hasn't called'. She knows he will call when he feels like it. The Hestia woman doesn't need constant validation from her man. She doesn't fence him in, and therefore she experiences more of her own freedom in the relationship. They help each other evolve. The Hestia woman has an innate respect for herself; therefore she calls him into his better nature. She contributes her clarity and wisdom, helping him see his patterns without making him wrong for being the way he is. She sees through his manoeuvring and impulsiveness and isn't rattled. He contributes his aliveness, creativity and spontaneity.

His rhythm in life is different from hers. It's fast, quick and often erratic. Hers is more organised, methodical and stable. When they wake up in the morning, he may want to make love, and she may want to get up and meditate, or take a shower and start her day. They could experience conflict if she feels pushed to join his rhythm. He has to be gentle with her and respectful of her. He can show her new ways by taking her along with him, but with a sense of fun and not as a way of controlling her. She must let him know if he becomes too pushy.

The woman who is charmed by a Hermes man who has not yet evolved out of his negative self-centred trickster into the archetype's more positive attributes should be cautious. Hermes' trickery and mischief are often admired in myth, but they're not so admirable in the modern-day man. He can charm his way into your bedroom and your heart, saying all the right words and meaning them in the moment. Hermes men have been known to walk away with women's fortunes, sleep with their friends and think nothing of it. And because his magic spell has them so captured, they forgive him again and again. So before you become mesmerised, find out a lot about your Hermes. Be an information gatherer. Ask him about his relationships with his mother, his father, his ex-girlfriends or wives. Watch out for his repeating patterns, and don't be in a hurry.

Hermes men sometimes complain to me that their Hestia women are not sexual enough. Hestia's sexual energy tends to lie dormant. For her, passion comes with the power of connection in the moment. Yet she does not always surrender to that passion easily. Hermes men, on the other hand, are very comfortable with their sexuality and have no shame or embarrassment. Together they have to be creative in finding ways to stimulate Hestia's eros. One of Hestia's gifts is knowing how to create a sacred space. One of Hermes' gifts is communication. Together they can 'plan to be spontaneous'.

Create a special atmosphere with soft music and candles. Start with a foot massage, or perhaps a full-body massage with special oils. Gentle caresses and kisses may help you get going. Hermes can wake up Hestia's Aphrodite with touch or with his voice, whispering in her ear; he has, after all, the gift of oratory.

Hestia and Hermes can create the most successful relationship of love, adventure and spirit-filled connection. Her ability to relate, listen and receive together with his erotic, creative nature that has no taboos allows them to be their natural selves with each other. She is the hearth and he is the fire. And if they keep working at it, the fire will keep them warm and will never go out.

Eleanor and Allan: Igniting the Hearth

My torn feet were touched by the golden dust of the road.
My fingers tore at the gold and silver gown that wrapped her
about. With a little whispering laugh she passed into me.
I was drawn into her and was healed.

– SHERWOOD ANDERSON, LOVE LETTERS

Eleanor is a feng shui consultant in New York City, single, and in her forties. She is genuine, soulful, a bit shy and has a natural elegance about her. Although she has been in several relationships, she has not made the plunge, and she had not been in a committed relationship for five years until she met Allan. He is a journalist who travels extensively. Divorced, with two sons in college, he is in his fifties yet looks forty – tall, lean, energetic and a bit rough around the edges. They met in June of 2001 at the opening of a mutual friend's art exhibit, where they struck up a conversation about art, spirituality and travel. Since both of them lived in New York

City, he called a few weeks later and they started to date. They found a comfortable level of conversation and a calm mutual attraction – none of Aphrodite's adrenal rush. It was a joyful and tender beginning – a Hermes man who has suffered blows and disappointments and grown from them, and a mature Hestia woman who has gone through her growth but never experienced a fully committed relationship.

He enjoyed her depth and the way she listened to him. She was stirred by his masculine way of taking charge, the way he openly expressed his strong feelings and his spontaneity. Passionate about his work, his friends, his art collections, his love for food and wine, he lived life with gusto. She was discovering a lot about him and asked about his past, his parents, his work, why he got divorced and his relationship with his sons.

He was generally the one to instigate their getting together. Typically, he would call at the last minute and say, 'Let's go catch a bite to eat and a movie.' They took their time to become intimate. Very much a Hestia woman, she was protective of herself and said she wanted to really get to know him first. She had been quite happy and content being single, so she wasn't about to stir the waters without knowing if this would be a safe harbour for both of them. She was developing a level of trust, and together they were nurturing the spark of their relationship.

On the morning of September 11, 2001, shortly after the terrorist attack, Allan called Eleanor to see how she was. A few hours later he called again to say he was being evacuated from his apartment because it was too close to the World Trade Centre, and he needed to come and stay with her – and bring his dog.

He arrived later in the day with the dog, a bottle of wine and a small suitcase and stayed a week. The horror of the day's events broke any barriers that had been between them. Frustrated by just watching the news and not acting, the next evening Allan decided to visit the site of the tragedy and write a firsthand account. With his indomitable mercurian charisma, he managed to get through the gates, Eleanor with him. Standing at his side that night in the rubble and smoke as he helped lighten the moment with hope and humour, the depths of her heart opened and she let herself be touched by the essence of this man. The rubble became the hearth because there was love and communion. That is the essence of the Hestia-Hermes connection.

The relationship progressed over the next year, the usual matters that surface in relationship showing up. A major issue for them was moving in together. Eleanor loved her home, which she regarded as her sanctuary, and moving in with Allan meant giving that up and adapting to a place filled with his energy and work. Interestingly, he was more eager for them to move in together than she, partly because he had found his home with her.

They considered selling his place and buying a new apartment together, but neither really wanted to do this, nor was it financially practical. Finally Eleanor came up with a workable plan that allowed her to retain her own space even while merging her home with his. She would move in with him and rearrange the bedroom to her own taste, establishing it as a feminine, nurturing haven. But she would also rent a studio apartment where she could have her office and stay there at night when she wanted to. She promised herself she would take her time carrying out this plan so she wouldn't experience a backlash from doing something that she did not wholly agree with.

She sometimes craves long, heartfelt conversations. But his attention span is shorter. He needs to be on the move and feels the most connected when he is engaged in something. Since he is unlikely to change, she has learned to seek that depth of conversation with her girlfriends, or allow it to happen spontaneously with Allan as it may.

She loves the sensual part of their relationship. He is very affectionate and tender, and she finds that she is comfortable with him in a way that is new for her. He has helped her accentuate her gifts, and bring out more of her youthfulness, letting her personality be freer and less conventional. She has often gone with him on his travel expeditions and has found herself doing things she had never dreamed of doing – canoeing, swimming in lakes and travelling in a hot air balloon. She has let go of the ideal image of who she thought the *perfect* man would be for her and found that what really matters is the enjoyment and aliveness she feels when she is with him. Her transformation has been very apparent and wonderful to behold.

She has softened him and eased his old feelings of not belonging. Allan's parents had not really paid attention to him, so at a very young age he had learned to survive on his own. She deals with his occasional venting about his parents, his ex-wife, his sons, or the challenges of his business by holding to a neutral place inside of herself and reflecting back to him another viewpoint. She is able to bring him back to his humour and creativity. By being who she is and allowing him to contribute to her life, she is helping him come home to himself. Her receptivity has been healing for him, since he was not allowed to contribute to his parents' lives. If Eleanor and Allan continue to grow together, their hearth will be ablaze with new territories to explore.

Hestia Speaks

*Benevolent and radiant Hestia, goddess of the hearth, show
me the way to you.*

Come sit in the circular temple of my heart
There by the blue lake
And be still, my love.
Let my calm waters
Wash away your fears,
Anxieties, and doubts.
Let me illuminate your soul
And bring comfort to your daily life.
Choose me
And keep choosing me
Over and over again.
I demand nothing,
I expect nothing,
But through me lies the fulfilment of all your expecta-
    tions,
The stillness where everything becomes one.
If you follow me
You'll find the deeper parts of you.
Seek not a man to choose you,
But choose yourself first.
Give yourself the golden apple
The golden rod
The silver cord
That leads you to your light.
Never let its flame go out
But be its emissary.
Own it and claim it
And let it pour through

Into your darkest corners.
You are safe in my love,
You are protected.
I am the openness you seek,
I am your doorway.
Come sit in the circular temple of my heart
And let yourself be calm.

Chapter 5

PERSEPHONE,
GODDESS OF THE DEPTHS

The Persephone Woman:
Innocent Maiden and Wise Queen

And did you get what
you wanted from this life even so?
I did.
And what did you want?
To call myself beloved, to feel myself
beloved on the earth.

— RAYMOND CARVER

The goddess Persephone has two fundamental aspects: As
the goddess of spring she represents innocence and youthfulness; as queen of the underworld, she is in touch with the
darkness and riches lying below the surface. So also, the
Persephone woman combines two states of being in herself.
She can be depressed and dark and then light, joyful and

uplifted. She is like a pure child and a wise woman all in one. Unconventional, receptive, mystical, youthful no matter her age, she may find herself equally present in two worlds – the world of her ego reality and the world of her unconscious. If, however, traumatic circumstances tear the thin veil separating these realms, she may lose touch with present reality, and her unconscious may flood into her conscious mind with all the unresolved feelings that have been lurking there – grief, separation, loss, fear, hopelessness – and she can be overwhelmed.

If she has not yet integrated her two worlds, she can appear ungrounded and girlish, going in one direction then another depending on how the wind blows. It may be difficult for her to make sense of the diverse emotions inside her, let alone have a healthy relationship with a man. Hopefully, her innate wisdom will counsel her to find a good therapist who can help her sort out those feelings and explore what is hidden underneath. If she seeks to work out her complexity in a romantic relationship, she will become needy and dependent on the man and create a lot of unhappiness for herself. There aren't many men out there capable of going to that depth with a woman. And anyway, you don't want your partner to become your therapist, nor should you expect him to.

In the myth, Persephone is the pure and carefree maiden who is forced in the most violent way to grow up. She is cherished and adored by her mother, Demeter, goddess of the earth, who provides for her every need. One beautiful summer day when Persephone is out gathering flowers in the fields, Zeus, her own father, and Hades, god of the underworld, conspire to have Hades abduct the girl and rape her and take her to live with him as his wife. Just as she bends down to pick an extraordinary hundred-petalled narcissus

– made specially to lure her – Hades emerges through a great fissure in the earth, seizes Persephone and descends with her to his realm.

In the abyss of the underworld, Persephone experiences devastation – which is what happens to us when we are suddenly snatched out of our own, sometimes utopian, reality into an unfamiliar world. Sometimes life demands that we grow faster than we can assimilate, and a gap in the development of our identity results. The Persephone woman's coping mechanism is to withdraw. She often looks as if she is not fully present and participating in the moment, that something else is holding her attention.

When Demeter discovers that her daughter is missing, she wanders the earth for days grief-stricken, not eating, not bathing, asking for Persephone everywhere. Finally, Hermes, always the messenger between the gods, reveals to Demeter what has happened. Then Demeter fights to get Persephone back, threatening Zeus that if he doesn't take action to retrieve her, she will bring famine to the earth. Zeus sends Hermes to tell Hades that he must release her. Persephone is ecstatic as she prepares to depart. Hades, however, craftily offers her some pomegranate seeds before she leaves, and she eats one. Though she has consumed nothing up to this point, by tasting even so much as a pomegranate seed in the netherworld she becomes bound forever to return. To bring peace to the realms, Zeus decrees that Persephone will spend two-thirds of the year – the seasons of new growth, abundance and the harvest – with her mother on the earth; and one-third of the year's cycle – the fallow winter months – she will live with Hades. Persephone then marries Hades and becomes queen of the underworld. Symbolically, she has matured – she has integrated her depths with her openness and lightness, her unconscious with her persona, and is ready to help others on their journeys through and out of the depths.

Another name for the young Persephone is Kore, which in Greek means both daughter and maiden. So also, the Persephone woman has a perpetual freshness about her, no matter how old she is. Think of Audrey Hepburn's youthful presence and adorable smile, with a twinkle in her eye, which remained with her to the end of her life. This youthfulness manifests in the inexperienced Persephone woman as the ingenue. On the one hand, she lives in an imaginary world; on the other hand, everyday reality never seems quite real to her. For this reason, she often doesn't plan for the future. She might be in a relationship or a job, yet she lives as if it is all temporary and she is waiting for someone to come and transform her life. Similarly, she may just let marriage happen to her. She might say yes to an offer of marriage and then become resentful and rebellious, for somewhere deep in her mind she has made only a partial commitment and thus feels as though she has been abducted. She is reliving the myth.

In the myth, Persephone is waiting to be reunited with her mother. Similarly, the Persephone woman may be looking for an all-accepting, all-embracing love outside herself. The Persephone woman seeks to please and be loved by others. Therefore, she risks compromising her own true wishes and needs in order to comply with someone else's. It's when she finally makes the connection with the Demeter within herself that she can feel fulfiled and experience herself as a whole person. What it takes to achieve that is learning to generously love oneself.

Somewhere in her unconscious the Persephone woman holds a negative perception of the male. In the myth, she did not bond with her father and her first experience with a man was abusive. Although the Persephone woman's situation may not have been so extreme, something happened to prevent her from experiencing her father as present on a daily basis and participating in her growth. Therefore she tends to attract men who are emotionally unavailable or even abusive – men who, like her, are young and live in a fantasy world, or tough, dark men, 'bad boys', who are drawn to her innocence and malleability. Or she may draw to herself men who have been controlled by their mothers and thus feel threatened by grown-up women; they find comfort in the less-experienced, girlish woman who won't challenge or criticise but will let them feel powerful and dominant.

She often cries after intercourse – a very natural reaction for a soul who is so open and willing to go deep. She can be flooded with all sorts of emotions and feel she is losing the self she has known. For this reason, a young Persephone woman might resist a sexual relationship, intuitively knowing it will open her up to unknown territory that she is not ready to explore. And she is wise to be highly selective about who she opens up with. However, when she is more integrated and assured of herself, she experiences her sexuality freely. She is able to let go and surrender to sex as a profound, even mystical, experience. Her innate passion can make her a very rich lover, and sex for her can be a rapturous, ecstatic experience that brings herself and her partner in touch in both body and soul.

The immature, girlish Persephone woman tends to procrastinate. She acts as if she has all the time in the world or as if someone is going to come to her rescue. She moves from one thing to another, taking up whatever calls her in the moment rather than staying a course and completing a project. She somehow manages to get things done at the last minute. In her womanly phase, however, she is a highly creative and innovative career person. She develops unique projects that have depth, and she can be unconventional in her choices because she is following the guidance of her internal queen. She is likely to choose a profession having to do with spirituality or psychology. A mature Persephone, with her sensitivity, can be a brilliant, empathetic psychotherapist. Or she may become an artist, a poet, or a psychic. Whatever she does will be highly individualistic and will contribute to other people's lives.

In her relationships with women, the Persephone type seeks a mother figure who has a strong personality and can protect and nurture her. She needs to be around women who can assist her in her growth and support her as she comes into her own. She also needs to cultivate relationships with her own Athena and Artemis aspects. She needs Athena's decisiveness and ability to focus, and Artemis's gift for trusting her own sense of direction and drawing boundaries. When these combine with the Persephone woman's native depth, she becomes a resource to herself and an extraordinary mentor for others. Conversant with the depths, and skilled in guiding others through their own internal labyrinths – from winter back to spring – she is indeed queen of the depths.

Her Strengths

- She is receptive and sensitive to other people's needs
- Her creativity leads her to develop deep and meaningful relationships
- She is in touch with the spirit and soul of life

- She tempers wisdom with compassion
- Her effervescent, youthful ways keep her young, no matter her age

Her Vulnerabilities

- She can be narcissistic and self-absorbed
- She tries to be all things to all people; she may try to please a man to gain his affection
- She can lose her sense of direction and make choices that lead her into destructive relationships
- Lost in the fantasy of what she wants, she may not be proactive in getting it and thus may feel like a victim
- Her vulnerability and emotional nature lead her to addictive behaviour

The Hades Man: Abundance in the Depths

Who drove her heart to me?
What impelled her spirit here?
Should I eat clay for bread?
Should I drink muddy water in place of beer?

— ISHTAR IN THE UNDERWORLD

The man who lives under the archetype of Hades has been dealt one of the most difficult hands in the archetypal deck. He is commander of his own world, but few come to visit it and its riches are locked away. If he wants a happier life he must draw upon other archetypes, such as Apollo and Hermes, who can give him direction and perspective. With their assistance he can bring in enough light and energy to unveil his riches and share them with others.

As god of the underworld, Hades is the archetype who helps us acknowledge death as an integral part of life. He reminds us of Socrates' advice: Practise death daily. These wise words refer not to physical death but to a willingness to let go of our reality of the moment so we can be open to fully experience the next moment. It is through these daily deaths that we grow.

Metaphorically speaking, the underworld is the realm of the unconscious, where our unwanted and unresolved feelings, the roots of our depressions and anxieties, reside. Yet the underworld is also rich – literally rich in gold, oil and gems; psychologically rich in creativity, strength and depth of character. That is why Hades is also known as Pluto, which means wealth. So don't think of Hades the god as a negative archetype. He presides over our periods of darkness, and it is in those times of enduring that we discover strengths and depths we may otherwise not know we have. To find them we may have to withdraw from day-to-day activities and spend time in reflection and deep listening.

The Hades man tends to be a loner – noncommunicative, moody, at times antisocial – withdrawing into his inner world, which becomes his refuge. He may be so wrapped up in that world that it is difficult for him to recognise other people's needs. As a woman in his company, make it your responsibility to get him to communicate. Sometimes he can't even articulate what he feels; if you want to know, you have to drag it out of him.

His introspective nature doesn't attract recognition, so he can remain unacknowledged for his gifts and have low self-esteem. His emotional aridness leads to a pessimistic outlook on life and chronic low-level depression. It is hard to be optimistic if you are looking out at life from a window in the underworld. The Hades man has to let his inner Hades show him how to see with different eyes and help him transform the base metal into gold, help him transform his morbid nature into the king that he is. The Hades man has his task cut out for him if he chooses to do his inner work. And if he does not do it, he feels stuck.

Tycoon William Randolph Hearst fits the mould of the Hades archetype. He was reclusive, extraordinarily wealthy and ruled over a newspaper empire. Ted Hughes, the English poet laureate, who was married to the poetess Sylvia Plath, a Persephone woman, and gifted at expressing emotions, is another such example. Filmmaker Roman Polanski takes us into worlds of darkness and emotional journeying in movies. In his movie *Chinatown,* the character John Huston plays is a Hades man.

The man living under the Hades archetype is one who seeks life and light. He can find these in Persephone. Profoundly attracted to a Persephone woman's youthful, light-hearted ways, he may try to possess them. Feeling that he needs her for his very survival, such a man can become obsessed with a girl and try to seduce her, even rape her. He can become very dependent on her. She, of course, draws him to herself by the power of the mythology playing itself out in her own unconscious. The more aware of her myth she becomes, the better she can take authority over it, riding the wave rather than being knocked under and carried by it.

My father was a man of the Hades archetype, combined with Zeus. As little girls, my sister and I would go and visit him after my parents had separated, and he used to fall into long silences and sleep long hours. I would try everything possible to liven him up, caressing him, being playful, saying anything to draw him out, but to no avail. He would be lost in his own abyss, sometimes staying there for days. Then he would have an outburst of excitement. He'd get dressed 'to the nines' – cologne, a fine suit, a silk tie – and be off to the nightclub life of music, women, Scotch, cigarettes and good food until sunrise, only to drop back into the abyss again when it was over. Such a chaotic cycle is a whirlwind with no end to it. Unless a man turns to his Apollonian spirit for guidance, his Dionysus will have his way with him. Hades men can be bipolar and express manic-depressive tendencies. To cope with their emotions, they may escape into alcohol to bring their feelings out, or into serial relationships, ending up in a relationship that is highly sexual and unconscious. Their inner instability creates a lack of self-confidence that makes it hard to succeed.

The surface world runs in time, while the underworld runs in eternity. To engage with the ordinary world, the Hades man must draw on and develop his Apollo qualities – his capacity for linear, rational thinking and organisation. He must develop his Hermes so he can give expression to his inner world and communicate it creatively.

Because of his ability to dive deep into the riches of the unconscious, a Hades man can be an excellent psychotherapist. Or he might turn to the church and become a priest or a monk, or work at a hospice and help others in the process of dying. Hades men can be brilliant artists with words, sounds, or images.

His Strengths

- Rich in his emotions and inner world, he never makes a dull mate and keeps the woman engaged
- He is highly creative

- He is sexy and passionate; he can make sex a rich and mystical experience
- He has depth and understanding of life and can assist others in finding themselves
- He looks for a stable relationship with a woman and likes to be head of the household

His Vulnerabilities

- He tends to withdraw and not communicate his feelings and be cut off from the world
- He can be swept away by unconscious sexual impulses with no sense of commitment
- He can be depressed and go into an emotional abyss
- He can be selfish and only concerned about what serves him
- He can be insensitive to his partner's needs

Persephone and Hades: Making Love Work in the Underworld

And they are gone: aye, ages long ago
These lovers fled away into the storm.

— JOHN KEATS

When a Persephone woman meets her Hades, she is taken by him in more than one sense. He entices her into his world; and she is equally attracted to his dark, contained, unconventional ways. She can be swept away in a moment. Their worlds match. He sees the territories they could explore together and wants to take her there. He permits her rich fantasies. Her emotions are allowed free rein. She often confuses love with passion and sexual desire. 'I'm so attracted to him and I don't know why'. Or, 'I can't seem to get away from him'. These statements reveal that she is 'driving under the influence' – the influence of her ignorance about what drives her.

At the beginning of a Persephone/Hades relationship, the sexual attraction can be passionate, exciting and all-consuming. The two of them can be caught in what turns out to be a pleasure trap. But their willpower can disappear and the structure of the relationship may grow chaotic, with very little planning or structure and a lot of flowing with the moment and getting lost in each other. There is no sense of time in the underworld. They may talk about their dreams, but nothing much will materialise unless they work at becoming more realistic.

It is essential that the Persephone woman and the Hades man ground themselves by engaging, separately, in some physical activity other than sex. This is especially vital for the Persephone woman, for she can lose herself in sexuality and in a man's energy. Involving herself in other pleasurable physical activities grounds her in her own energy. Yoga, a Pilates class, a dance class where she can move creatively with music, hiking, or any inspirational activity that allows her to reconnect herself with herself will empower her.

If she is still the maiden wanting to be saved, she may see him as her saviour. However, he is anything but her rescuer. As in the myth, he merely takes her into the confines of his own dark world. Moreover, he can't help her out of the labyrinth he brings her into. He takes no responsibility for the effect he is having on her. He might as well be saying: I didn't force you to fall in love with me, so now learn to live with me. At his worst, a Hades man can be cruel and destructive, even abusive. He may withhold love and affection, and withhold money and caring as well. One Persephone woman confessed to me that her husband would lie in bed next to her reading the paper, and the more she wanted him, the more he refused her. She found this so erotic that she climaxed on her own.

He also becomes very attached to her. He likes her to feel dependent on him and encourages it. It makes him feel powerful; after all, he is a king. She is the captured maiden who can be on the receiving end of his outbursts. On the other hand, he can be seductive and erotic, which hooks her. So she is trapped; her extraordinary gifts remain undefined and unexpressed. If he is willing, he could encourage her to explore her potential and anchor her strengths. But he is stopped, fearful of her power and the possibility that she might leave him. That is the myth.

When a Persephone woman makes a Hades man the centre of her life, she is chaining herself to the floor of her own underworld. Her real goal is to get out of hell! Once she has restored herself, she can freely choose to be with this man. Then, and only then, can she and her Hades man start to experience a conscious, fulfiling relationship. She may even be able to assist him. But first she has healing work to do: channelling the richness of her being to resource herself rather than her partner, educating the maiden part of herself, bringing comfort and love to that tender aspect of herself so she can mature.

If you are caught in the dark side of a Persephone-Hades relationship, you must take a deep breath, and a still deeper exhalation, and know that there is a way out. In the myth, Demeter is working hard to bring her daughter back to earth. Demeter represents the warrior-mother in you, your higher self who watches over you, nurtures you, is devoted to you. Zeus, king of the gods, sends Hermes to fetch Persephone. That Hermes is none other than your own powerful spirit, bringing you solutions so you can come back to the light. It can guide you to the person, or persons, who can help – a wise friend, a therapist or counsellor, or perhaps a spiritual mentor.

You need to incorporate your Athena, the aspect of yourself who knows how to take charge – including charge of your unconscious behaviour – and take the steps to heal your emotional world. She can tap your ability to stand up for yourself, to become autonomous. Join forces with her. And you need to invoke your Artemis nature and put her to work building boundaries for yourself and helping you move steadily toward your goal. Both of these archetypes can show you another way to be.

I have a lot of the Persephone archetype in me. Some of my patterns regarding men began at a young age and I am still healing them. My father would explode in anger at my mother, and as a little girl I was scared of his abusive masculine power. My mother never retaliated, and neither did I. We all learned to withdraw to give him space to vent. My sister and I often heard the words: 'Leave your father alone; he is in a bad mood'. That was a wise choice, yet living in apprehension of his bad moods opened up the psyche to fear. Fear, however, can be replaced with strength, and accessing your strength is the key to your liberation. My mother one day summoned up her strength and told my father she was leaving, that she was taking her two daughters and moving out – an extraordinary act of courage in Athens in the sixties, and against all conventions, especially as she had no job or income of her own.

Although she left and gloriously survived, she stayed tied

to him emotionally. She worked through her anger and her pain; she blamed herself for having chosen him. When he died, she found that she missed him because, underneath all the anguish, she still loved him. She passed away just three and a half months later.

The mythic Persephone was raped. Even if the modern Persephone woman isn't raped physically, something happens to her that feels like rape. The world may have been too harsh with her, or perhaps she had to grow up too quickly. She carries old wounds, and she needs to take steps to heal them.

One of the ways she can heal is by being held lovingly by her partner, so she can feel love and trust not just emotionally but in her body. Then she can begin to open up to the extraordinary riches hidden in her heart. So her man may need to take the time to really be with her in a gentle way. One woman I knew had her partner hold her and kiss her until she could let the love in. Now, tenderness is not a natural expression of the Hades man. But there must be some way in which he is comfortable expressing his affection. What do both of you find moving? Music? Reading to each other? What activities other than sex can you do together that can help the two of you bond and heal?

Even so, the Persephone woman needs more attention than the Hades man is prepared to give. And if you start demanding that he should be a certain way or are critical of him, he will retreat even more, because he is already critical of himself. So you need to take care of yourself and build inner strategies to handle his withdrawn, pessimistic moods and his emotional dryness.

If, for example, you are invited to a party and he is in one of his antisocial moods, there is no reason why you shouldn't go on your own or with a friend and enjoy yourself. He probably doesn't want to go out because his inferiority pattern is surfacing, and he is already visualising himself having a bad time. However, the fact he doesn't want to go out has nothing to do with you. If he is still in that bad mood when you come home, let him be; fighting about it is not an answer.

Avoid the trap of feeling you have done something wrong when your Hades-archetype partner withdraws. You may want him to at least tell you what is going on inside him, and the fact that he says nothing may seem like a rejection. You might think, 'If he loved me, he would do what makes me happy, he would adjust'. But he can't. Dealing with a Hades man who has done no work on himself can at times feel literally like hell. You might be operating under the fiction: I see the potential in him and if I give him time and nag him he will change. The reality is: He is who he is; the only way he'll grow is if you say, 'I am staying in this relationship if you are willing to grow, and if not I am moving on' and mean it. In the long run, he needs to choose to do his inner work – and you have to decide if you want to stay in the relationship if he isn't willing to change.

Paradoxically, the best way to understand a Hades-driven man is to distance yourself from him. If you are so wrapped around him that you only see him up close, within the context of the underworld, you'll be caught in judgment and the frustration of not being able to change him. Viewing him from a distance, you can see the patterns playing out in his life. On the one hand, you'll feel compassion for him. On the other, you'll find yourself ready to untie yourself from him and experience your own freedom.

Remember, in the myth Persephone does come out into the light. And she moves with ease between the underworld and the earth. It is her freedom that allows the two of them to join at last as king and queen.

The mature Persephone woman has accessed her soul and knows its depths. From that vantage point, she can even help her Hades man transform some of his darkness. She has learned not to give in to his negative cycles. She becomes his light-bearer and can actually lead him higher, not saving him but rather, by her behaviour, helping him construct connections to the outside world.

If both partners in a Persephone-Hades relationship are willing to do a lot of introspection and psychological healing, they can have an extraordinarily rich relationship in which they acknowledge and even enhance each other's gifts. Together they may start projects that have quite an impact on other people's lives, sharing those gifts with the community. One such couple I knew – he was a director and she was an actress – started their own theatre company. It was rich with new plays, workshops, inventive productions and talented people who found in it a place to express their gifts. The atmosphere popped with creativity – unorthodox, unconventional and cutting-edge in every way.

When Persephone and Hades harness their energies together, magic happens. Their playfulness and sensuality run high, and the potential of manifesting happiness and fulfilment becomes a reality. But it takes choosing a direction and a method to structure their rich dream world.

Alicia and Adrian:
The Courage to Get the Hell Out of There

Alicia was in her late twenties, beautiful and sensual with long, dark hair and an expressive face that could simultaneously convey innocence and depth. Her father was a successful movie producer in Hollywood, a powerful, controlling man. Growing up in a Hollywood family, she had chosen acting as her own career and played small parts on stage. She loved live theatre. Though she dated occasionally, lately she had been annoyed by the shallowness of men her age and had found herself wishing for a deeper connection with a more mature man.

She had a magical, innocent way about her. I am sure that's what first caught Adrian's attention. Adrian was tall, lean, handsome and in his mid-forties – a scriptwriter and one of her father's close colleagues. He had never married but had been in his share of relationships, and he was not particularly looking for one at the moment he met Alicia.

They met at a party for the opening of a play Alicia was in. They chatted casually, but underneath the talk was a palpable sexual chemistry. Alicia was intrigued. Although Adrian was much older than Alicia, she felt more comfortable with him than her peers.

As fate would have it, the playwright invited Adrian to the following Sunday's matinee performance and the discussion of the play afterward. Adrian accepted, knowing it would be a good opportunity to connect with Alicia again. She didn't know he was going to be there and was pleasantly surprised when he showed up. He invited her to dinner at a French bistro afterward, where it was evident to both that the attraction between them was serious. For Alicia, the world around her faded and Adrian's presence became all-consuming. She was fascinated by his mystique, and his attention was an aphrodisiac. On the way to the car he put his hand on her neck and drew her to him and kissed her. That was that. She couldn't wait to fall into the arms of this man, who seemed to offer all she thought she wanted. He was so seductive – his disarming way with words, his provocative air of command.

The affair evolved rapidly, and when Alicia's father found out he was outraged. He even threatened to disown her. He warned her of Adrian's bad reputation in love affairs, but she was deaf to his remarks. Very shortly, she moved in with Adrian. They were swept away by the sexual passion that erupted between them. They spent long hours in bed – making love, sleeping, talking, listening to music, reading. They went for walks at the beach and sometimes Adrian went into the kitchen and cooked up his speciality, Thai coconut-shrimp soup; but mostly they ordered food in and ate in bed. Little by little, she was drawn deeper into his world until she knew herself only in relationship to him. Losing herself in the eros that encompassed them was in itself not so detrimental; the problem was that she had no self of her own to return to, no anchor. He became her anchor.

When they were not spending time with each other, he was busy with a script for a movie. He was happy having her close to him while he worked – she might be out on the deck reading a novel – but he never encouraged her to audition for a part or pursue her own dreams. She avoided her father and felt less and less inclined to spend time with her friends. He listened to her daydreams about what she wanted to do, but if she took a step toward making it happen, he would carefully distract her, asking her to proofread the scene he'd just written or taking her to Catalina Island for a weekend. She liked pleasing him and doing what he wanted. Gradually, he became more autocratic, and she became more dependent on him.

When his script went into production, she went on location with him. To her shock and amazement, he began to spend time with the supporting actress, who was ten years Alicia's senior, on the excuse that they were working out the details of her part. But clearly his attention was starting to split. He dismissed Alicia's pleas to pay more attention to her as a girl's whim. She felt taken for granted, miserable, desperate that she might lose him, and stuck. Then they would spend a passionate evening together, and she would be hooked again. There was something about the way he kissed her and made love to her that made her succumb to him completely.

One rainy morning they had a terrible fight, and she decided not to go with him to the filming site that day. As Adrian drove off, Alicia noted between her hurt and her fury that the rain had grown to one of the heaviest downpours she had ever seen. An hour later the phone rang. Adrian's car had collided with a truck and been flipped over at the side of the road. Adrian was badly hurt, with a broken hip and a broken leg and contusions. He was in the hospital for several weeks, and then the two of them returned home.

Alicia became 'nurse' to a very grumpy man who could no longer make love to her. He grew depressed and was becoming addicted to painkillers. She had very few people to turn to. She had reached the bottom of her underworld. And she didn't know that she had a choice.

Then, one night when they were watching television, a commercial came on for an investment company that advertised itself as offering clear solutions. The commercial ended with the words: 'Don't be a victim. Choose wisely. Invest for your future; you are worth it'. The words were like a searchlight that caught her mind in their bright beam, and in that brief moment everything shifted.

She looked at this man lying in bed, dark, humourless, holding on to her as she was holding on to him, and she felt a cold wash of estrangement sweep over her. For the first time in the year and a half they had been together the sea was parting, and she felt a glimmer of her own self. She fell asleep that night with tears streaming down her cheeks.

She didn't know where the courage came from, but the next morning, while he was still asleep, she quietly packed her things and wrote a note. She wrote that she was sorry to leave this way, but she wasn't strong enough to tell him in person she was going, and she had to leave him if she was ever going to find herself. She asked him to not seek her out, to give her time to find her way back to the surface without interference. And she added: 'You showed me a world that I thought only existed in plays. I'm sure one day I'll look back and see the value, but right now I am spent.'

Her transition back to her own world happened gradually. She reconciled with her father, returned to her acting, healed her bruises and surfaced into the light.

Sometime later she was in another play, and on opening night she received a beautiful vase of lilies of the valley and a note: 'The times I had with you were the only happiness I have ever known. Love, Adrian'. She thought to herself: an interesting choice of words; he could have said, 'The times *we* had *together* were the only happiness. . . .'

Ah, she smiled to herself, clearly she was over him. Her breath didn't catch, her thoughts didn't go to him. She knew she was unhooked, she was free – and very, very grateful.

Persephone Speaks

Persephone, beloved goddess of spring and queen of the underworld, tell me where I can find you and how I can better learn from you. . . .

You can find me dancing with my playmates
In the luscious meadows

Filled with flowers of every kind and colour –
Roses, crocuses, beautiful violets, irises,
Hyacinths and narcissus.
I am slender and beautiful – maiden among the
    immortal gods,
Brilliant and adored.
I am Demeter's beloved and cherished child.
Carefree and innocent,
I live in my eternal spring, and
Everything around me is always blooming!
'Til one day Hades, the awesome god of the under-
    world,
And my father's brother,
Came from under the earth and snatched me away
    from my happiness.
I was raped and abducted,
I screamed and wept.
No one heard my cries or rescued me.
My mother grieved and wept
And wandered on the earth.
I lived in hell.
It seemed like an eternity.
I lost all time.
I ate nothing. I spoke to no one.
I lived without hope or light,
I lived in bondage.
I gave up hope of
Ever seeing my mother's face again.
She never stopped plotting,
She never gave up.
She used her goddess power and
Threatened famine on the earth.

My father, Zeus, succumbed,
And sent the beautiful Hermes
With his winged sandals and chariot
To find me,
And my heart leapt for joy.
The day had come to see the earth again,
My mother's face, the flowers and my playmates.
As I stepped into Hermes' chariot,
Hades, who was bereft to see me go,
Handed me a pomegranate seed.
I thought nothing of it, I took it and ate it,
Not knowing that this act
Would forever bind me to return.
And then I was back in my mother's arms,
Her tears of joy and mine blending into one.
Oh, to see the light of day again
And touch the earth with my slender feet!
Helios, god of the sun, shone brightly in our hearts.
But I had tasted the food of the underworld.
I had no choice.
It was arranged
That every spring, summer and fall
With my mother I'd remain
And I'd spend the winter months with Hades.
I am not afraid anymore
I am not in grief.
I bring my light into the underworld
And help others
Who, like me, come and fear death.
I love my husband, Hades,
Not as my abductor but as the man I chose to marry.
I've overcome!

My abduction became my resurrection.
I'm fearless over death,
Eternal and forever young,
The woman and the maiden all in one.
You'll find me in the dark and light domains of your
    heart.

Chapter 6

ARTEMIS,
THE INDEPENDENT GODDESS

The Artemis Woman: Focused Huntress

Zeus has made you a lion among women.

— HOMER

'I can take care of myself' – this is the conviction that res-
onates in the Artemis woman. Her independence of spirit,
her feisty confidence and her laserlike ability to accomplish
what she sets out to do are what distinguish her from others. She does not define herself by her relationships. In fact,
she can stay happily single, and she tends to choose her
close companions carefully.

The mythology tells us that on one of his many extramarital escapades, Zeus pursued and impregnated the nymph
Leto. As her time of delivery neared and she sought a place
to give birth, Leto was turned away by everyone for fear of

the wrath of Hera, Zeus's rightful wife. Finally she came to the sunny, magical island of Delos. There she gave birth first to Artemis, who immediately became Leto's midwife, helping her mother through the difficult birthing of her twin brother, Apollo. Thus Artemis was worshipped in ancient Greece as the protectress of women in childbirth.

When Zeus sat three-year-old Artemis on his knee and asked what she wanted for her birthday, she requested a bow and arrow, a pack of hounds, a tunic short enough to run in, mountains and wilderness where she could hunt, and eternal virginity. Her request was granted. As goddess of the moon, she roams the forest at night. As guardian of the animals, she also hunts them, pursues them and slays them. By day she dances and bathes with her chosen companions, the daughters of the god Oceanos.

She is fast, vital, instinctual and moves like a gazelle. If you want a project done on time, give it to an Artemis woman. She's very much a here-and-now person. Untrammelled by her intellect or emotions, she directs all her energy to accomplishing the task – not thinking about it or analysing how she feels about it, but taking action. On the other hand, her emotional dryness can lend her an air of masculinity. In fact, Artemis is the most androgynous of the goddesses.

The young Artemis woman fits the classic picture of the tomboy, disliking girlish clothes, preferring to be 'one of the guys'. She might not develop an interest in men until later in life. As an adult she might wear little makeup and dress in basic, practical clothes. Yet she carries herself with a confidence that is attractive, even striking. And when she does dress, she can look stunning. Hers is a raw, essential beauty, not fashioned to please someone else.

She treasures her independence and her privacy. She is the woman who gladly spends a summer alone in a Rocky

Mountain cabin, letting her soul merge with the land, the sky and the buffalo. Her pure instinctual nature feels more at home in nature with the animals than in the city interacting with people. Her strength is derived from the boundaries she erects around herself. Greta Garbo's famous delivery of the line, 'I want to be alone', in *Grand Hotel,* captured the voice of Artemis. When you feel an almost instinctual urge for solitude, Artemis is working in you. We must listen to ourselves as our soul calls us for inner, private time. That is how we travel to the unexplored domains of our consciousness where we find the gift of an exhilarating freedom – freedom from the opinions of others, from what binds us from our past and from what is expected of us in the future.

The Artemis woman pursues her goals with the same confidence, focus and impeccability that characterise the goddess as she hunts a deer by moonlight. We see this in her even as a little girl – the concentration and courage of young gymnasts such as Nadia Comaneci and Kerri Strug. She thrives in competitive environments and loves to rise to meet a challenge – Amelia Earhart, the first woman to fly solo across both the Pacific and the Atlantic, was unquestionably an Artemis. The sports arena provides an ideal environment for her energies – tennis champions Venus and Serena Williams are elegant examples of Artemis women. The Artemis woman also loves to fight for a cause, aligning herself with the 'voice crying in the wilderness'. Anthropologist Jane Goodall, who quit conventional society to spend four decades studying chimpanzees in Tanzania, has now turned her attention to speaking out for protecting endangered species and the environment.

Tenacity and fearlessness run in the veins of the Artemis woman whether she is on a mountain climbing trip or taking on the challenges of saving the Alaskan wilderness, protecting the whales from extinction, arguing for women's rights, or developing microcredit unions for third-world women. Activist Erin Brockovich roused a small town to successfully challenge a huge utilities company for polluting the local water supply. In the movie *Bend It Like Beckham,* Jesse pursues her passion for playing soccer in the face of her British Indian family's outrage and eventually wins a university sports scholarship – and her family's support. Independent, outspoken actress Angelina Jolie chooses feisty, action-oriented roles that suit her Artemis personality. And of course the warrior princess Xena, female action hero of television fame, is the Artemis archetype writ large.

The Artemis woman may apply the same cool-headed aim and concentration to finding a male companion. An Artemis friend once told me, 'I knew that if I wanted a relationship with a man, I needed to go hunt him down and bring him home. He wasn't going to be knocking on my door'. That is exactly what she did. She started the hunt methodically, making a list of the qualities she wanted in a partner, meeting men on the internet and inviting the possible candidates for coffee, for half an hour only; that was the agreement. If there wasn't a rapport within the first five minutes, she didn't even stay for coffee! She wasn't about to take care of the guy's feelings. She proceeded through the selection process in a remarkably detached way. If she liked a man but he didn't call back, she didn't fret; she just went on to the next one. One day she met a man she really liked, and he was also very drawn to her. Even so, she didn't get too excited. She kept dating others until it was obvious that this man was the one for her. That was not until she had had try-out dates with forty men! They have now been together for five years, but she still has her own apartment because, a true Artemis, she is very protective of her own space.

The man who is a good match for her has a creative and aesthetic nature and is intellectually compatible. She should avoid men who are dominating or want to be the centre of her life. She needs to find a kindred spirit, her male counterpart – like the goddess's twin brother, Apollo. Although she may lack in emotional intimacy, if her eros is tapped, her instinctual, animal nature will come to the forefront, and she can be a wild and exciting partner to be with.

In the story of the Trojan War, Artemis demands the literal sacrifice of Iphigenia, daughter of the Trojan hero Agamemnon, in exchange for fair winds that will carry the Greek ships to Troy. According to one version, Iphigenia dies; according to another, Artemis saves her at the last minute and makes her one of her priestesses. Similarly, the Artemis woman can be ruthless with her own feminine nature, sacrificing her emotions to accomplish a larger goal. She can be equally demanding of others. If she's your boss, she will demand the same precision and excellence from you as she embodies herself. As a mother, she can be like Artemis's she-bear, devoted and protective, raising her children with loving discipline.

The goddess Artemis could be merciless and quick to cruelty. When the nymph Niobe insulted Leto, Artemis, helped by Apollo, killed all twelve of Niobe's children as punishment. The Artemis woman, too, keeps her figurative bow and arrow in hand, and if you cross her – whether you are a lover, a colleague, or a friend – you may become her target. She keeps her anima – her soulful feminine – under wraps, and thus tends to dominate men. She can be harsh, bossy and even emasculating. If her partner doesn't have a healthy sense of self-esteem, he can fall under her shadow. And if he betrays her, she can be quick to cut off the relationship for good. Once, when the goddess Artemis was bathing in a forest pool, the hunter Acteon peeked at her and was entranced with her beauty. Discovering that he had invaded her privacy, she felt violated and insulted and her merciless aspect came to the fore. She splashed him with water, which turned him into a stag, and his own dogs hunted him down.

Her spirit of competition, too, can undermine her relationships with men. In the myth, Apollo challenged his twin to hit a target far out to sea. She rose to the occasion and fired off an arrow that struck the target – which turned out to be her lover, the hunter Orion. Perhaps it's no accident that both Acteon and Orion were mere mortals; the lofty goddess they admired turned out to be not only beyond their reach but also the cause of their deaths.

To temper her fiery nature, the Artemis woman may embrace her Demeter aspect to develop her compassion and capacity to nurture both herself and others. Her inner Aphrodite can show her how to open up to her feminine receptivity, allowing her partner to take care of her. She will invite her to set aside her bow and arrow for a little while and put on a silk scarf.

Her Strengths

- She accomplishes her goals with focus and impeccability
- She is self-reliant
- She is proactive in making her life work rather than waiting for others to make it happen for her
- She has a great sense of adventure and fun
- She knows how to enjoy her solitude, which connects her to her soul

- She loves, appreciates and occupies her body freely and is very comfortable in her sexuality
- She can be an invigorating and reliable partner

Her Vulnerabilities

- She can be cut off from her emotional nature and therefore find it a challenge to connect and relate to others
- She can be uncaring and aloof, even cruel
- She can be critical and judgmental of others if they don't meet her standards
- She can be so goal-oriented and structured that she might miss the joy of spontaneity
- Her relationships can become too platonic, ending up a friend and companion rather than lover with her mate

The Apollo Man: Noble Man of Reason

I am the eye with which the universe
Beholds itself and knows itself divine.

– SHELLEY, 'HYMN OF APOLLO'

The last time I was in Greece I visited the island of Delos, home of the god Apollo, and for the first time I understood the magnificence of this god and his attributes. Soaked in clear Mediterranean sunshine – not a tree in sight – even today Delos has an aura of grandeur. In ancient times, this sacred island, with its splendid temples, fountains, market-place and theatre, would have been a cosmopolitan town offering all the amenities of the day. The harmony and proportion of the site reflected the qualities of the god himself. The excellence that permeates Delos is the excellence that governs Apollo. He is the god of the sun and second most powerful god of the Olympic pantheon after his father, Zeus. He has everything to do with law and order, reason and logic, music and architecture, sports and the arts. In Giraudoux's play *Apollo of Belzac*, Apollo says:

> From the line of my shoulders, the geometricians derived the idea of the square. From my eyebrows the bowman drew the concept of the arc. I am nude and this nudity inspired in the musicians the idea of harmony. . . . From the eyes of beauty poets derived the idea of death. But the feet of beauty are enchanting. They are not feet that touch the ground. They are never soiled and never captive. The toes are slender, and from them artists derived the idea of symmetry.

Apollo's myth tells us that he was birthed on Delos, the second-born after his twin, Artemis. His first nourishment was not his mother's milk but the nectar of the gods, fed to him by the ancient goddess of prophecy, Thetis – foretelling his role as the god of prophecy. He killed the great she-dragon called Python at sacred Delphi, regarded by the Greeks as the centre of the world, and took over her temple and its functions. His oracle, the Pythia, an elderly woman, would go into a trance and deliver prophecies and judgments from Apollo. The rules inscribed on the temple walls convey the moderation and control that characterise this archetype:

> Know thyself
> Nothing in excess

Curb thy spirit
Observe the limit
Hate hubris
Keep a reverent tongue
Fear authority
Bow before the divine
Glory not in strength
Keep women under rule

The man who comes under the Apollo archetype is likely to have a handsome, clean-cut appearance. He is bright, keen-minded, steady, polished. There are no extra papers on his desk, his tools are stored in an orderly fashion and even his closet is tidy and organised. He brings a standard of impeccability to whatever work he does, and keeps his distance from conflict and entanglement. He is the man who follows the rules and excels.

The god Apollo is an archer, and he instills in the Apollo man the ability to aim for his target in life and succeed. If he is encouraged and supported as a boy (by his parents and mentors), he is likely to do well at everything. He is the A student who goes out for track and field, plays trumpet in the school orchestra, is student body president, and is headed for a university education. The Ivy League suits him to a *T*. He is willing and eager to engage in long studies and hard work in pursuit of a career. A true son of the patriarchy, he may succeed in his father's business.

Whether he is an architect, a businessman, an accountant, a banker, a doctor, or an airline pilot, he brings clarity and vision to what he does. Men who exemplify the Apollo archetype include astronaut and U.S. senator John Glenn, the first American to orbit the Earth and, at the age of seventy-seven, the first to return to space travel as a senior citizen;

painter David Hockney, described as the most highly publicised artist of the late twentieth century; actor Tom Cruise, whose charisma and genius for success make his movies regular box-office hits; actor Leonardo DiCaprio, who blends emotion, intensity and reality into consistently stunning performances and is equally committed to protection of the environment; and golfer Tiger Woods, youngest person to win the professional golf Grand Slam and the only pro to hold all four titles at once.

Every resident of Olympus has a built-in flaw, and for Apollo it's relationships. A true son of the patriarchy, he has rejected the feminine aspect within himself – in Jungian terms, his anima – and women reflect this outwardly as rejection. Suffering from a syndrome of unrequited love, he was snubbed by nymphs and human women alike, and apparently had connections with no goddess except his sister, Artemis. He is entranced with the beautiful maiden Daphne, whose hair is in disarray, and he wonders: If she is so beautiful like this, how much more lovely would she be if her hair were carefully arranged? She runs from him and he chases after her, declaring his love and begging her not to flee. In desperation she prays to her father, the river god Peneus, who changes her into the laurel tree. Apollo, grieving that he cannot have her as his wife, chooses to wear laurel leaves as a crown – later the emblem of victory for winning athletes.

When he falls in love with the Trojan princess Cassandra, he decides to negotiate. He promises her the gift of prophecy if she will love him back. He keeps his promise but she doesn't, so he curses her: You'll see the future but no one will believe you – the Cassandra curse. He, on the other hand, suffers from what we could call the entitlement curse: When his offerings of love to other women, such as Sybil and Marpessa, meet with rejection, he is baffled – he is so sure he should be loved because of his magnificent intelligence, beauty and many gifts. Passion and a deep connection of the heart seem to elude him.

Similarly, while the Apollo man can excel at everything he undertakes, he is unable to transfer the same skill to the domain of the heart. He is often out of touch with his own emotions, and he tends to keep other people at a distance. He may apply the same rational methodology to obtaining a mate as he would to creating a project or constructing a building. He will look for a wife who is the perfect fit with the lifestyle he seeks – someone compatible with his family and colleagues and who has similar tastes. He might not be in love with her, but he loves what she represents, and he wants her because she completes his world.

In his darker side, the cool-headed, rational Apollo man can be arrogant and self-serving. It's all about him. He can have an inflated ego and feel he is above others, and he may care more about things and ideas than about people – that is, until things don't turn out the way he wants them to, or life in some other way humbles him. This may be the only way the Apollo man's heart can evolve.

Cruelty can also show up in Apollo's psyche. In the myth, a satyr challenged Apollo to a musical competition, and Apollo, who appointed himself as judge and jury, declared himself the winner. Since the bet called for the winner to do whatever he wanted to the loser, Apollo flayed the satyr – a cruel manifestation of his intolerance with being challenged. If as a child, an Apollo man is not encouraged to develop his gifts, but is criticised or humiliated, he may turn against his noble nature and be filled with hostility. If his mother was unemotional and distant, he may show that hostility to women and aim to wound them because he himself is wounded. If you're ever with such a man and the hostility is aimed at you, it is good to remember that, deep inside, the man himself is suffering.

His cruelty may show up as passive-aggressive behaviour. His potentially sunny nature becomes clouded and twisted in on itself. He may withhold affection, withhold attention, or become a man of few words as a way of controlling people. This man, so sensitive to beauty and grace, may never pay you a compliment. You might be wearing a lovely dress and look stunning as you go out for an evening, and just as the two of you depart he'll say something that crushes your joy. I once dated a man like this who I knew was in love with me as I was with him. Early in our relationship he went on a trip abroad, and when he returned I joyfully asked if he had missed me. He replied with a certain malice, 'Quite frankly, I didn't even think of you.' I was hurt but said nothing. But as this mean-spiritedness kept occurring, I withdrew from the relationship and never regretted it. To deal with such manipulative behaviour you must bring forth your Artemis and come back to him with strength and confidence. Only then you will have his respect.

The Apollo archetype is one of the dominant patterns in Western civilisation. Both men and woman may find they have spent all their life following the Apollonian social norm, obeying the shoulds of society and family, confined within the straitjacket of Apollo. The archetype will run us, until we decide to take it on and redirect it. Once the Apollo man looks to his spirit for guidance, he will find the courage to evolve. By developing his inner Hermes – younger brother to Apollo – he will give himself permission to be freer, more spontaneous and break through the confines of conformity. He may also choose to spend time with his Dionysian nature. At Delphi, for the three winter months of the year, Apollo would withdraw and the god Dionysus, another brother of Apollo, would take over. So it is with the Apollo man. Listening to Dionysus, he will get out of his rational mind, start to celebrate his life and do things just for the fun of it. As he incorporates these other aspects of himself into his way of being, he discovers how to be free in spirit even within the Apollonian structure of his life. As he evolves personally, so does the archetype.

The Apollo man who has learned to include his heart in his life will let himself fall in love with a woman for who she is, and outward appearances and forms are less important. This openness will attract to him his perfect match, his archetypal twin, the Artemis woman. As the Apollo man aligns with his higher nature, however, his inner light will illuminate himself, his relationships and the world around him. All his gifts will shine, and he will bring clarity to all he does and everyone he meets.

His Strengths

- He stands tall and brings steadiness to the relationship
- He is focused and disciplined and able to aim and succeed at his goals
- He loves and appreciates beauty in all forms
- He is a loyal and devoted mate
- He is not a television surfer, he likes to watch one programme to the end
- You'll never have to pick up after him, he is orderly and tidy

His Vulnerabilities

- He tries to control life's flow, leaving nothing to chance and lacking spontaneity
- He is cut off from his emotions and lives in his head
- He places too much attention on appearances and form
- He has a sense of superiority and entitlement
- He can withhold love, communication and can be passive-aggressive
- He can be self-absorbed, insensitive to other people's needs and narcissistic

Artemis and Apollo:
A Joining of Kindred Spirits

He showed me lilies for my hair,
And blushing roses for my brow;
He led me through his gardens fair;
Where all his golden pleasures grow . . .

He loves to sit and hear me sing,
Then, laughing, sports and plays with me;
Then stretches out my golden wing,
And mocks my loss of liberty.

— WILLIAM BLAKE

It is true that both the Artemis and Apollo archetypes run the risk of being too self-reliant and independent to develop a love relationship. In the mythology, the women Apollo pursues reject him, while Artemis keeps company with her nymphs and is hardly interested in men. Yet the mythology also reveals that these two are in fact more closely bound to-gether than any other gods. They are the only twins among the Olympians. They complement each other. Artemis is goddess of the Moon, Apollo is god of the Sun. She is at home in the wilderness and protects the wild animals; he in-spires the building of cities and as sun god owns a herd of cows. She dances freely with her nymphs; he methodically composes music and plays it on his lyre.

Archetypally speaking, the Artemis woman and the Apollo man have twin souls out there. If they are lucky they will find their soul mate – someone who, like a mirror, brings to light a part of themselves they otherwise might not see. When they meet, there is often an instant recognition. Each is the perfect match the other has been looking for all his or her life. They balance and complete each other. Not that the relationship won't have its challenges – like other couples, they must work to make the relationship work. But the Artemis/Apollo relationship holds a potential for compat-ibility unmatched by any other archetypal relationship.

One actor-actress couple that exemplified the Artemis/Apollo couple was Jennifer Aniston and Brad Pitt. They seemed to have a deep bond of friendship and com-patibility. However, sadly their focus on their separate ca-reers and so much time apart cost them their romance.

When I talk to Apollo/Artemis couples, I often hear state-ments like: 'I've felt comfortable being with him from day one', 'I felt so at home, I could totally be myself with her', 'I married my best friend', or, 'He is the brother I never had, only I get to have sex with him, too.' Apollo men who have Artemis partners often say that they love always knowing where they stand with her; there are no hidden agendas. In one such marriage I attended, I heard the most beautiful vow exchanged: that they would be transparent with each other;

whatever they might be feeling, they would reveal those feelings to each other in the moment. This practice has granted that relationship tremendous breathing space, since nothing is stored up, unspoken. Since their hearts are so open to one another, their relationship is alive and their love flows.

The Artemis woman may meet her Apollo man over a project at work, or on a biking trip or on the ski slopes or at the gym – somewhere that engages the love they share of the outdoors or accomplishing a goal. The attraction between them has none of the male/female seductive games à la Ares and Aphrodite. They just enjoy each other's company and do everything together. He finds her refreshing, clean-cut and direct. He loves her focus, her authenticity, the way she sources herself without leaning on him, the way she makes decisions without emotion. To him this is her true beauty. His admiration and devotion to her may be reminiscent of how a younger brother adores an older sister. She, in return, loves the way he treats her as an equal and doesn't try to dominate – this couple, for instance, is likely to split their financial responsibilities fifty-fifty. His dependability and calmness soothe her fiery side. She admires his mind, his cultivated manner, his appreciation of beauty and love of culture. She may find him inspiring.

Karen Blixen, whose story is portrayed in the movie *Out of Africa,* was a turn-of-the-century Artemis woman who married to find adventure. She moved to Africa, where she ran a coffee farm single-handedly and fell in love with Denys, a kindred spirit who loved Mozart, adventure and his freedom. In one scene, when they are out on safari and falling in love, two lionesses charge them, one after the other. They stand side by side, twinlike, as each kills one of the beasts with a single shot – Karen first. It's not long afterward that they spend the night together and start a long-term relationship.

They may bond at first because of their common interests and physically driven energy, taking pleasure in doing
things together and enjoying a good-bye kiss. But after a
while this friendship may naturally evolve into their living
together and eventually, marriage. He may be the one who is
keener to move the relationship forward. Apollo, after all,
wanted to bond with certain women and chased after them.
She, on the other hand, may be more cautious, despite the
connection she feels with this man. Bonding with a man
challenges the Artemisian belief that she can take care of
herself. Her independence is so priceless to her that she naturally resists. The inexorable pull toward love and bonding
is moving her out of her comfort zone of self-reliance, and
she may experience a lot of conflict in having to give up her
personal space and ways of doing things to include someone
else. Opening up to parts of herself that have been shut
down to intimacy with another can make her feel excruciat-
ingly out of control. However, when she finally gives herself
permission to let go and embrace the relationship, she will
find great satisfaction and safety, for she will feel she is coming home.

To others, their relationship may appear distant, for this
is not a demonstrative couple that touch a lot or gaze across
the room at each other with bedroom eyes. On the contrary,
they are the couple that after the dinner party is over, one
gaze between them and they know it is time to go. They
don't linger. Both are more practical, thinking about what
time they have to get up the next morning. They live life for
a purpose rather than pleasure. The Apollonian motto 'nothing in excess' fits both of them.

When the Artemis woman comes home after a day's
work, she often needs to consciously change gears, switching
from the get-it-done energy of the working world to a softer,

more receptive aspect of herself. Getting out of her work clothes into something comfortable and sensual, taking a bath, dancing, listening to music, taking a walk in nature – all of these can slow her down so her feminine nature can come forward – in other words, put down her bow and arrow and become goddess of the moon. This is where her Aphrodite can help her. If she doesn't make this shift, she and her Apollo partner may remain like two buddies, doing things together and enjoying each other's company, and miss out on the passionate, erotic aspect of their relationship. And if this continues for a long time, they might find themselves letting sex go altogether.

If they lose the eros between them, the Apollo man may find himself looking for that passion in an affair with another woman – just as Apollo pursued a nymph. And if his Artemis woman is emotionally distant and out of touch with her intuition, she might not even suspect it. Yet even if he has an affair, he will most likely return to the marriage because he gravitates to its form and security.

If she finds out about the affair, her ruthless, vengeful side may emerge. She will accept no discussion or negotiation but will simply cut him off, pack her bags and leave. On the other hand, if her Hera aspect keeps her in the relationship, or her Demeter makes her stay for the sake of the children, she will face the challenge of finding the compassion to forgive him.

Two other challenges they may have to face in the relationship are her potential for controlling his actions and whereabouts, and becoming competitive about their achievements and who gets more recognition. Unless talked about, these challenges will create friction in the relationship.

If their shared interests include the pursuit of a spiritual goal, another dimension to their relationship will blossom.

Meditation or prayer or the study of the spiritual path together will create a depth that binds them. They will bring that spiritual energy into their sexual relationship as well, which will make their union more fulfilling.

Karen and Kenneth: Overcoming the Seven-Year Itch

Karen met Kenneth at a key moment in her life. She had recently ended a relationship because, as she said, 'The guy was not bringing enough of a heart investment to the table.' When she asked a counsellor how much she should compromise to make a relationship work, the counsellor responded, 'Until you feel you are compromising yourself.' Those words were a wake-up call. She realised she had indeed been giving away too much of herself, and she was done with it. In honour of her thirty-second birthday, she decided to return to the single-girl, independent lifestyle she had always loved.

Three months into her new way of life, she met Kenneth, a good-looking, forty-year-old Phoenix architect, at a friend's birthday party. Just two days later they ran into each other at the high school track and fell into an effortless conversation about running shoes. When they chanced upon each other at the health food store the next day, Kenneth asked her to accompany him on Friday to the opening of a downtown arts centre he had designed. He says that even on this first date he kept getting the strong sense that this was the woman he wanted to spend the rest of his life with. She was the first woman he'd met whose attention was not all on herself, so there was room to be with her. There was space around her, and it was comfortable and breezy.

A week or two after the opening, Karen's work as a free-lance nature photographer took her away on an assignment. When she returned, she found a beautiful book on design waiting for her with a little note from Kenneth saying how much he had enjoyed being with her and invited her out for dinner. After dinner they went to his apartment, which she loved as soon as she entered. His aesthetic sense and good taste were manifest everywhere, and it struck her that his space was very much a personal statement. He was very attentive; she felt that when he looked at her he was really seeing her. Both of them said later that the romance really started that evening. They began spending a lot of time together, travelling and enjoying each other's company. And he loved her playfulness, her sense of freedom and her exotic, bohemian ways. She found him generous and inspiring to be with. She loved to listen to him – she would always learn something new. He encouraged her in her work; she blossomed around him. She even loved his dark, brooding side and found it mysterious.

About a year later Kenneth left for a two-week trip to Nairobi. When she didn't hear from him the entire time, Karen decided to end the relationship then and there. Why couldn't he have phoned even once? Finally she got a call from him; he was at Kennedy airport and was on his way home. She told him that the relationship was over; her Artemis had been violated and she wasn't about to negotiate.

The first thing he did when he got back to Phoenix was to go visit her. The photographs of the two of them were now missing from her apartment. She said she had ripped them up. He apologised without defending himself and explained that phoning from Nairobi had been nearly impossible. And he made a new promise to be devoted to her and to the relationship.

A few months later he proposed, and they got married. He was, she said, steady as the North Star, self-confident and directed. They took several trips, including a canoeing adventure in Canada, set up a home together and began planning for a family.

Seven years and three children later, parenting had become a major part of their lives. They were impeccable parents. Karen threw herself into the role of a mother with the same energy and attention that she gave to her career. And Kenneth wanted to give their son and two daughters the best start in life possible. Seeing no way to do it all, Karen 'reeled herself in', as she said, so she could serve her family. She gave up photography – for now, she told herself.

But suppressing her self-expression and freedom came at a cost. She became controlling and bossy with the children and Kenneth. When Kenneth wanted to do something on his own she would protest, 'You can't go do that and leave me alone with three kids.' Worse, during the seventh year of their marriage, Karen was told she had breast cancer, and the diagnosis became a wake-up call. Her Artemis love of space, solitude and freedom was going completely unaddressed. She realised she had to take care of herself, and the cancer treatment itself – a lumpectomy and chemotherapy – meant she had to allow other people to take care of her as well. Her drive for perfection softened. She began to see that she did not have to be the perfect mother. And she knew she had to revert her consciousness to a positive focus.

Meanwhile, Kenneth was feeling confined. He felt like a parody of himself. The Apollo archetype was pushing on him – too much form, too many controlled activities – and his true self was ready to evolve. He began having wonderful dreams of flying. On the other hand, he found himself noticing other women and with pangs of guilt asked himself if he wanted an affair. He asked himself the question: Where is the freedom in the middle of the family structure? He was looking for a way out without destroying what he treasured.

For both Karen and Kenneth, form had overtaken spirit. Both of them wanted more freedom. Shortly after Karen's treatments were finished and she was declared 'clear' of her cancer, they sat down to talk. While both of them wanted more freedom, neither wanted to leave the marriage or be less present for the children.

It requires a lot of insight and skill to break out of an old form that's not been working into a new expression without breaking a family and a marriage. Because of their commitment from the beginning of the marriage to be honest with each other, they didn't hide their feelings and courageously communicated how they felt. They decided to seek spiritual counsel. Kenneth saw that the freedom he sought was inside himself, and not in an extramarital relationship. Karen realised that her freedom was in relaxing and letting go of the controlling ego. They decided to start a new chapter of their lives called 'moving to L.A'. Karen had always wanted to live in Los Angeles because of its arts culture, and Kenneth would commute from Phoenix and be with his family Thursday evening through Sunday.

Kenneth had to give up the idea that being a good father meant being there for the children every day. And Karen had to surrender her ambition to do it all perfectly. She says, 'We don't always eat home-cooked meals; we eat out a lot. My house is a mess on weekends. But I'm happier than ever and truer to myself than ever.' The children are happy and filled with the love of their parents. Karen said to me, 'I could hardly believe that I was really going to leave Phoenix. But you know what? My forty years in the desert are now over!'

They are a joy to be around. They have revitalised their relationship, their family structure, and I can tell you that they are now truly living happily ever after.

Artemis Speaks

I am the great goddess of the hunt,
I am the huntress of the wild,
Virgin goddess of nature's wilderness,
Defined by no relationship,
Confined by no bond.
I honour the feminine in all things.
Pure, untouched, my feminine spirit is intact;
It has never been and never will be violated by a
    man.
I belong to no one but myself.
I am whole and complete within myself,
The untameable spirit
That is the essence of the primitive feminine.
You will find me running in the woods
With my nymphs.
I love those wild animals
That have never been
Subjugated by man.
The games of childhood and the chaste thoughts of
Adolescence belong to me.
I am the invincible virgin,
Fierce and beautiful.
I am tall and lean,
Swift and masculine.
You will see me with my
Gazelles, my hounds, my wild beasts.

My passion is for the freedom soul
That I find in nature
Communing with the animals –
The rivers, the brooks, the forests and the meadows.
I'll show you how to use my silver bow and arrows
And aim for your target
And kill your prey.
I am ruthless and strong.
Be not afraid of your power in me.
I am your guiding presence.
I love my women friends, my nymphs,
I play with them,
I hunt with them,
I dance with them.
Nature is our kingdom.
My alabaster flesh is my wedding gown,
My bow and arrows are my crowns.
Follow me and you will
Feel the power of your body,
Your speed like a gazelle,
Your strength like a bear,
Your pride like an eagle.
I punish those who violate my boundaries,
I am merciless like a bear whose cub is threatened.
Come find me.
You will still be in the world
But will be like my deer,
Dancing free, defined by no one,
Confined by no one.

Chapter 7

HERA,
GODDESS OF MARRIAGE

The Hera Woman:
To Wed or Not to Wed,
There Is No Question

Who can find a virtuous woman?
For her price is far above rubies.
The heart of her husband doth safely trust in her . . .
She will do him good and not evil all the days of her life.

— THE BIBLE, PROVERBS 31:10–12

The Hera woman is born to be a wife. She has marriage on
her mind and in her heart. She is looking for the man who
will be her husband, the partner with whom she can build a
family and a foundation. Once she finds him, she will be
loyal and devoted – committed to making the relationship
work at all costs. She finds fulfilment and completion only

in marriage and identifies herself in relation to her significant other. Depending on her psychological makeup, she
will either be fulfiled in a partnership, where she will flour-
ish as the powerful queen at the side of her king, or she will
follow the course of the myth – wooed and seduced, then
betrayed and disempowered. If she follows the myth's full
cycle, she will renew herself, regain her power and then
bring that fullness back into her marriage.

Hera's myth tells us much about her psyche. Born on the
beautiful island of Samos, one of the six children of the
Titans Cronus and Rhea, she, like all her siblings except her
brother Zeus, was swallowed by her father right after birth.
When at last she emerged, she had grown into a young girl.
Zeus, who had overthrown Cronus and become ruler of the
gods, was consumed with passion for her on Olympus –
there are no prohibitions against incest. He created a violent
rainstorm, transformed himself into a cuckoo and sought
shelter at her bosom. She took pity on him – and then he
revealed himself in his real, magnificent form, and ravished
her. They got married and, according to Homer, their honeymoon lasted three hundred years.

The Hera woman longs to find her male partner and
knows that she must be married to fulfil her destiny. She
hears the calling of marriage and wants to follow it. If she is
in a relationship with a man who is reluctant to move forward, she may press him to marry her. Bernard Shaw captured this aspect of Hera in his play *Man and Superman:*

Tanner: The trap was laid from the beginning.
Ann: From the beginning from our childhood for both
    of us – by the life force.
Tanner: I will not marry you. I will not marry you.
Ann: Oh, you will, you will.

Tanner: I tell you, no, no, no.

Ann: I tell you, yes, yes, yes.

Tanner: No.

Ann: Yes. Before it is too late for repentance. Yes. . . .
You do not love me.

Tanner: It is false. I love you. The life force enchants
me. I have the whole world in my arms when I
clasp you. But I am fighting for my freedom for my
honour for myself one and indivisible.

Ann: Your happiness will be worth them all.

Tanner: You would sell freedom and honour and self
for happiness?

When her man asks her to marry him, the Hera woman
feels she is in heaven. Her wedding day is the happiest day
of her life, the day she fulfils her destiny. Marriage is cele-
brated almost universally as the most pivotal transition in a
woman's life, as well as in a man's, when they join as one.

As a wife, she supports and takes care of her husband and
loves to take care of his every need – from seeing that his dry
cleaning is done to seeing that his favourite food is in the re-
frigerator to looking good for him to creating a home that
runs efficiently so he never has to worry about the details.
She is the woman who will take sides with her husband before she takes sides with her children. He comes first – and
she comes first for him as well. Their lives revolve around
each other. Even if she works and has her own career, the
marriage is still the centre. She is fulfiled in that role, confident in herself and in her feminine power. His masculine
power then matches and balances her. This is the true
Zeus/Hera union, the essential marriage. They are equal, neither is superior to the other, but they bring each other their
unique gifts and a deep honouring and respect that enhance

each of them. The two can be dining alone and yet feel like royalty because each views the other that way. She knows he is her king, and he makes her feel like a queen. They protect, nurture and support each other. Paul Newman and Joanne Woodward seem to embody the partnership of Zeus and Hera, as did Robert and Ethel Kennedy.

The Hera woman who is still single and has not found her mate feels incomplete. Although she may enjoy her work and be involved in the community and have good friends, she will feel that something is missing, that she hasn't fully lived because she has not been married. In such cases, something is holding her back. She may be holding such a romanticised, idealised image of who her husband should be that she doesn't recognise him when he comes along. Or she may have had a dominating father who, 'devoured' her, and her deep psyche will not allow her to find her mate for fear of being overpowered by a man all over again. The single Hera woman would benefit a lot by doing her inner healing work – examining her beliefs and fears and breaking them down – becoming her own partner first. She must unravel the way the myth plays out inside of her before she can manifest what she wants outside. Once she sees how and why she holds herself back, she will be free to have what she wants.

In the myth, once the honeymoon was over, Zeus got the three-hundred-year itch and proceeded to let his libido run away with him, having affairs with and impregnating goddesses, nymphs and mortals alike. Humiliated and powerless, Hera became the jealous, angry queen of Olympus, taking revenge by turning Zeus's girlfriends into cows, flies, bears and even an echo.

The Hera woman is so identified with marriage that she finds her identity through it and doesn't have a solid sense of herself otherwise. She runs the risk of putting up with mistreatment from her husband out of fear of being alone, especially if she is not financially independent. Her husband may start to have affairs, or ignore her or hurt her feelings or even abuse her, but she will submit and endure. Friends may tell her to get out of that bad marriage, to leave him, yet she finds that inconceivable. She may retaliate by making a scene or, as in the myth, she may withdraw and lick her wounds till they are healed. But she will not walk out of the marriage.

The theme of the betrayed wife has played itself out in women's lives throughout history. A classic example of a Hera woman is Jacqueline Kennedy Onassis. Regal and beautiful, as First Lady she created beautiful environments at the White House that supported John Kennedy's presidency, overseeing every detail and imbuing it with her own graciousness and elegance. Like Hera, she was first lady of a state, loved and admired, and she endured her husband's well-known infidelities. And when he was assassinated, she bore the aspect of Hera Chira, Hera the Widow; the archetypal image of Jackie in a black veil at her husband's funeral is forever imprinted in our consciousness.

When her husband betrays her, the Hera woman almost inevitably reacts with the goddess's jealousy and rage, and becomes bitter and resentful. She can become obsessive, checking up on him, reading his emails, checking his personal belongings, following his every move. She may become a nag and a shrew, entering a permanent state of war with her husband, obsessed with destroying the other woman or punishing him. The legendary Medea of ancient Greece, the woman who kills her children in order to destroy her husband, who leaves her to marry another woman, is an extreme example of the Hera woman taking revenge because of her pain and anger.

One of the most inspiring moments of Hera's myth occurs when she decides not to put up with Zeus's infidelities any longer, leaves him and travels to her sanctuary at Evia, planning never to return. Zeus tries to make her jealous by staging a mock wedding with a marble statue of a woman, and Hera is so amused that she decides to come back. But she returns a different Hera. She has reclaimed herself and her power. She has become Hera Telia – Hera the Complete, the essential wife, no longer bound by the role of wife.

Hera's story is about the regaining of feminine power within the patriarchal structure. In modern society we are still working out this archetypal pattern – the wife finding her individual power within the marriage. In many cases, she never does. Growing up in Athens, I saw numerous such marriages. The man would often put the woman down, shutting her out of decision making and financial matters, saying her place was at home with the children and taking care of the household. These women felt hurt and resentful, yet they were stuck in the relationship, unless they had means of their own. This is one form of the suppressed Hera – the woman who is confined within a marriage and sees no possibility of breaking away. In many countries today women still suffer under this patriarchal suppression. And even in the United States, where the women's movement has brought about many changes, many women still struggle with not knowing how to untie the knot of an unfulfiling and oppressive marriage. I have often contemplated what courage and faith it took for my mother to leave my father, deciding she would no longer put up with his infidelities and bad temper. She raised the bar for women of her time, and certainly for my sister and myself.

The most significant step a married Hera woman can take is to decide to turn her attention to herself and discover her power and, maybe for the first time, a relationship with herself. This step can be challenging. It might mean leaving the marriage entirely. In a letter included in a report conducted by *Cosmopolitan* magazine in the 1980s, one woman describes how she found her way out of a miserable marriage:

> I had been programmed in my typical middle-class Catholic upbringing to believe that the ultimate life goals were being a faithful wife and a devoted mother and having a beautiful suburban home. No divorce. No working mother. I was miserable. What could I do? Since I had six years of solid secretarial experience behind me, work seemed the most logical place to start. . . . I went to call on a prospective client, one thing led to another, and suddenly this nice 27-year-old wife and mother found herself in bed with someone else's nice husband. . . . Six months later I left my husband and moved in with my lover. I am still with him now.

Another option is to take a sabbatical from the marriage. A friend of mine who was married for thirteen years and found herself in the rut of being a wife decided to go to Paris for six months, live with a friend and study art, which was her passion. She had saved money so she could make the trip. The creative spark recharged and reinvigorated her – and also rekindled her heart with the love she originally had for her husband. When she returned, she got a job in the local art museum. She said to me, 'It was the scariest thing I'd ever done. But once I took the first step toward myself, it was as if all the goddesses had lined up behind me to help me.'

In the movie *Shirley Valentine,* a woman whose life and marriage have gone stale takes a trip to Greece. She has a brief love affair with a Greek man, but in fact, she says, her real romance is with herself. Her husband goes to Greece to bring her home. In the final scene, he walks right by her without recognising her. She has rejuvenated herself and the movie hints that by doing so she will now rejuvenate their marriage, too.

The letters in the word 'Hera' are the same as in the word 'hear', reminding us that the Hera woman needs to listen to her heart and find the courage to do whatever it takes to keep her heart liberated. And that is often a heroic act. But after all, 'Hera' is the feminine form of 'hero'. She should not stay in a marriage that doesn't satisfy her emotionally. The marriage vows say, 'Till death do us part', but isn't death the absence of love? And why should anybody stay in a loveless marriage? Yet the Hera archetype can so blindfold a woman that she cannot see herself other than as a wife – 'I am a wife to someone, therefore I exist' is what she believes. Even if she leaves one husband, if she hasn't established a relationship with herself, she'll only repeat the pattern, until one day she takes off the blindfold and sees the world in a brand new way, realising that before she can belong to someone, she has to belong to herself.

When a woman leaves the structure of a marriage that doesn't work, she begins to release herself from her beliefs and fears about needing to be bound to another. The collective wife consciousness is deeply rooted in her, and when she decides to leave, a chorus of voices rises inside her, crying, 'You can't survive on your own; you'll be eaten alive' – which is the core belief in the Hera psyche. She may be in her forties, or fifties or sixties, and never have experienced herself as a person in her own right. And when she leaves, it is a scary, vulnerable time. She hardly recognises herself, and the world doesn't give her any recognition either. Familiar ways of doing things fall away and she has not yet acquired new ones. I once heard Jane Fonda speak openly and candidly on this issue at a conference. The daughter of a powerful man, she has been married to three strong men – the third, Ted Turner, a true Zeus. When she left her marriage with Ted Turner, she said, for a period of time she could hardly speak; she was reconstructing her identity.

Women have told me that they felt like they couldn't breathe as they took this first step on their own, that they felt paralysed with fear. If she calls on her Athena to infuse her with a new purpose and her strength when she thinks she has none, and her Artemis, who can give her boundaries, she can do it. In Ibsen's play *A Doll's House,* Nora feels trapped in the empty shell of the role of the wife. When she decides to leave, her husband says, 'You are a wife and a mother before everything else', to which she replies, 'I don't believe that anymore. I believe that I am a human being just as much as you are.' It is that belief and trust in herself that she needs to summon up to get her out the door.

As a Hera woman you might find that you become more of a partner than a lover to your husband. At the end of the day you end up going to bed, reading your favourite novel while he's reading a new business book, have a kiss good night and turn over and go to sleep. You'll see him flirting and having too many late dinners with clients or starting to have an affair. For this reason it is essential that you keep your Aphrodite close by. Hera, after all, borrowed Aphrodite's magic girdle so she could charm Zeus. A friend of mine who has been married for twelve years made a commitment early in the relationship to not let her wifely role ruin her romantic life, so she decorated their bedroom in a sensual and luxurious way. She told me, 'We need to keep our lovers' side nurtured. Having my Aphrodite bedroom is a trigger.'

A woman who has an active Demeter aspect may marry and have children, but the marriage may not be fulfiling to her Hera aspect. If during her marriage she meets another man who is more her true mate, she may agonise, feeling pulled between the two archetypes. Should she stay in the marriage or leave? It all depends on which archetype is stronger in the moment. Frieda Lawrence wrote about her marriage with D. H. Lawrence:

> When I first met him, and with absolute determination he wanted to marry me, it seemed just madness and it was – I was older than he, I had three children and a husband and a place in the world. And he was nobody and poor. He took me away from it all and I had to be his wife if the skies fell, and they nearly did. The price that I had to pay was almost more than I could afford with all my strength. To lose those children, those children that I had given myself to, it was a wrench that tore me to bits. . . . [Yet] everything seemed worthwhile, even trivial happiness; living with him was important and took on an air of magnificence . . . as if a big wave had lifted us high on its crest to look at new horizons.

It is this marriage wave, with its ups and downs, which the Hera woman rides throughout her life and it brings her the fulfilment she seeks.

Her Strengths

- She is fully committed to partnership in marriage
- Her presence is majestic and she carries herself with strength and confidence
- She wholeheartedly supports her husband in his work and helps him succeed
- She attends to her husband's needs and cares for his well-being
- She creates a beautiful home
- She thoroughly enjoys her role as a wife
- She manages the household and family and her world with ease

Her Vulnerabilities

- Her jealous nature can get the best of her
- If she's betrayed, she can give in to anger and resentment and lose her sense of self
- She can overidentify with being a wife and lose her identity
- She can be proud, full of herself and feel she is above others
- As a mother she can tend to side too much with her husband rather than her children
- She can be overly possessive and controlling

The Zeus Man: Born to Lead

His legs bestrid the ocean; his reared arm
Crested the world; his voice was propertied
As all the turned spheres, and that to friends;
But when he meant to quail and shake the orb,
He was a rattling thunder.

— WILLIAM SHAKESPEARE,
ANTONY AND CLEOPATRA V.2 82–86

Power, leadership and acquisition are what drive the Zeus man. Zeus's symbols are the eagle and the thunderbolt, and like an eagle going after its prey, the man living under this archetype sets his eye on what he wants and goes after it, whether it is a woman, a company, a bank, a network, the next deal, or the next political office. He needs his kingdom and his queen by his side – and often he needs to have his love affair on the side as well. His drive to acquire exactly what he wants and his gift for wielding authority put him naturally in positions of leadership, where he thrives. He is every Caesar and every leader who has governed, not by brute strength but by strategic use of might. Like Zeus with his thunderbolt, he can be ruthless with his power, or he can use it for justice and the good of all. Either way, his impact is enormous.

When we look at the mythology of Zeus, we understand this archetype's deep-rooted ambition to survive through power. Zeus's father, Cronus, had swallowed each of his older siblings as they were born, for fear that they would grow up to challenge and defeat him. When Zeus was born, Rhea substituted a stone wrapped in swaddling clothes for the infant, and Cronus unsuspectingly swallowed it. She then hid the child in a cave on the island of Crete. Once he was fully grown, Zeus came up with a plan to defeat

Cronus. He liberated his siblings, and he and his brothers fought and defeated Cronus and the other Titans. He was the supreme strategist. He freed the Cyclops and the giants from the dungeon under the earth where they were imprisoned in exchange for their assistance. And finally he fought Typhon, who wanted to destroy the world. Justly so, after leading the overthrow of the Titans, he became ruler of the world. His brothers Poseidon and Hades took jurisdiction over the seas and the underworld, respectively, and Zeus presided over the earth and the sky, the divine and human worlds. He brought law and order and made sure the other gods did not abuse their powers. His very name means 'to shine', and his presence illuminates the world.

Zeus's gift for sovereignty makes this man a figure of stature in his world. Even as a child he expresses his will, crying and demanding to be heard when he wants a toy or food or something is not being done the way he likes it. As he grows up, his drive to achieve and his natural leadership abilities emerge. He may be president of the student body or the fraternity. He's the guy who gets every girl he wants – until he wants a wife, and then he strategically chooses one. He will pick a career that can lead to a prominent position. For example, if he chooses marketing or finance, he will be on the track for the CEO. We see his drive in the head of state, in the Hollywood producer, in the ranching mogul in Montana. Like the sky god himself, his vision is large. He thinks of the big picture. He's not just about the paycheck, he's about creating.

These men are masterful at the game they play. If their power is used for the good of all, they are visionaries and are highly protective of the institutions they run. One such man was Winston Churchill, who in one of his most famous speeches inspired the British to battle in World War II. Like

Zeus, he then became the great diplomat who brought the forces together to fight the great battle.

> We shall go on to the end. We shall fight in France, we shall fight on the seas and oceans, we shall fight with growing confidence and growing strength in the air, we shall defend our island, whatever the cost may be, we shall fight on the beaches, we shall fight on the landing grounds, we shall fight in the fields and in the streets, we shall fight in the hills; we shall never surrender, and even if, which I do not for a moment believe, this island or a larger part of it were subjugated and starving, then our empire beyond the seas, armed and guarded by the British fleet, would carry on the struggle, until, in God's good time, the new world, with all its power and might, steps forth to the rescue and the liberation of the old.

This is a big god with a huge persona. Zeus men are lovers of the big life. They love to entertain, to be lavish, to show off their wealth and share it. They can be generous with their friends and give generously for philanthropic causes as well. One of Zeus's names is Zeus Xenius, which means Zeus, the Hospitable One. He was also called Zeus Philius, the good friend, and Zeus Plusius, the one who has wealth and riches. The man who channels his energies in the positive flow of the Zeus archetype is a great husband and a great boss. He can be a pillar of society who has riches and knows how to use them.

In the myth, Zeus is a protective and generous father and provides for his family. He is a proud father, too, and loves his children. When Dionysus's mother dies during pregnancy, he sews the fetus into his side and carries him to full term.

He gives his daughter Athena complete control of the lightning bolts and trusts her with the aegis. He settles a conflict between his sons Hermes and Apollo, and the two brothers can become friends. So also, as a father figure, the Zeus man is dynastic, the paterfamilias. He is Big Daddy in *Cat on a Hot Tin Roof*. He is Marlon Brando in *The Godfather*. He is Nelson Rockefeller. As a father he favours the children who obey his wishes and execute his orders. And he is sure to distribute his wealth accordingly when he passes on.

For centuries, the Zeus archetype has stood for the patriarchal order, and under its dark aspect the feminine has suffered. Under his dominating power, women have fallen into a subservient position.

The man who has not evolved the archetype in himself can be an oppressive husband, boss, or father because he is disconnected from his high nature. He excludes anything to do with his own anima, his internal feminine side, his feelings, his vulnerability, his receptivity and the only way he feels he can handle and grasp the feminine is by possessing it and controlling it.

If the Zeus man engages the dark side of his archetype, greed and ego will lead him to make unwise choices and ultimately self-destruct. He won't see that he is driving himself into a wall because he's blinded by ambition. He thinks he is invincible and will be spared, and he is deaf to the warnings of those around him. He will then find himself joining forces with his brother Hades, in the darkness of the underworld.

This type of man loves to seduce and ravish a woman. He has a big sexual appetite. He will wine her and dine her and buy her lavish presents. And many women are drawn to their power and the sense of security they feel with them. This is the kind of man who, when he has his arms around you, you will feel that he can make the earth shake for you. He is attracted to beautiful women who make him look good. Acquisition of different women feeds his ego and sense of power. Consider, for instance, real estate multimillionaire Donald Trump, married and divorced twice, who is always seen with a beautiful woman at his side and has become the producer of the Miss Universe pageant.

In the myth, Zeus uses the great skill of transformation in order to seduce the women he wants. He changes into a swan to seduce Leda, into a cuckoo to conquer Hera; he appears as a bull to Europa and to Danaë as a golden shower of rain, and for Io he becomes a cloud. So it is with the Zeus man; he will find just the way to charm the woman he is after, until he has made her his own. In Mozart's *Don Giovanni,* when Don Giovanni sings his famous aria, 'In Italia, mille che', it is the Zeus in him boasting about his many affairs in different cities. But although this man might have numerous liaisons, when he's with you, you feel you're the only one.

The Greek tycoon Aristotle Onassis was a Zeus whose life was about the power of acquisition and being one up with his competitor, Livanos. Although he was married to Livanos's ex-wife Tina, he had a well-publicised love affair with opera star Maria Callas. And after his wife Tina died, he made a move that would enhance his power on the world stage – he pursued and seduced one of the world's most famous women, Jacqueline Kennedy, and married her.

With Hera it is different. She is an extension of Zeus's being. Since he has repressed the feminine within him, by uniting with her, he unites with the receptive and nurturing qualities of the feminine. This marriage to the feminine is vital to his success. It balances him, completes him. His importance in her life enhances and expands him, and he can gracefully and easily arrive at the top and, with her, govern. Even if she is in the background, her presence is essential to him. As one friend told me, 'I used to date lots of beautiful and sexy women. But with her it was different. I didn't fall in love with her, but I wanted her presence in my life. Her strength and honesty made me feel this was a woman I could go the distance with. Later, after we got married, I really got to love her.'

Zeus had seven official wives, the last being Hera. But he had countless affairs with other goddesses, nymphs and mortal women with whom he fathered numerous children. He considered this behaviour as his prerogative and disregarded Hera's feelings completely.

King Henry VIII of England followed in Zeus's footsteps by having six wives and changing them according to his needs. As portrayed by Shakespeare in *Henry VIII*, he praised his first queen, Catherine of Aragon, his wife for twenty-four years, yet he divorces her because she has not borne him an heir:

> Go thy ways, Kate. . . .
> Thou are alone –
> If thy rare qualities, sweet gentleness,
> Thy meekness saint-like, wife-like government,
> Obeying and commanding, and thy parts
> Sovereign and pious as could speak thee out –
> The queen of earthly queens.
> She is noble born, and like her true nobility she has
> Carried herself towards me.

Nevertheless, he defied the Pope and established a separate church for England so that he could have his way and marry Anne Boleyn.

Because these men hold the reins of power, they resist change until something happens that makes them question their invincibility – a personal illness, the sudden death of a loved one, a wife walking out on them, a business deal collapsing. For example, Aristotle Onassis's son was killed at the age of twenty-three in a plane crash, and Aristotle never quite recovered from the blow.

The Zeus man is driven by a primordial instinct to survive by claiming and asserting his power. He works with all his might to make sure he is on top. He creates successful alliances and strategies. He negotiates, he seduces, he plots. He has a vision of the whole plan he must execute. He's a master manipulator to the degree that those around him do not know they are being manipulated. If, however, he loses that vision of the whole and becomes self-serving, he creates his own downfall. The many American CEOs who fell out because of greed and deceit are the ones who allowed the dark side of the archetype to take over. They compromised every value and principle because they refused to accept defeat and went against the primary principle of leadership – in the words of Winston Churchill: 'The price of greatness is responsibility'. For a Zeus man to lose is the ultimate humiliation and vulnerability, for he has no way to deal with it. He feels crushed. We often see such men felled by a heart attack, symbolic of the opening up of a heart that has been closed.

When the Zeus man incorporates his Poseidon aspect, he will gain emotional depth. He will be even more seductive because he'll have not only power but he'll also have access to his feelings, and can be more effective in reaching people. And as he embraces the gifts of Zeus's other brother, Hades, he will open up to a richer inner life, and he will learn to see life from many dimensions.

His Strengths

- He thrives in positions of power and leadership
- His is a passionate and seductive lover
- Larger than life, he is generous with friends and family
- He can be a good provider for his wife and children
- He is able to inspire and move people to carry out a plan for a cause
- He is powerful, intelligent and a man of vision

His Vulnerabilities

- He can be a philandering husband
- He can be domineering and controlling and want things to be done his way
- His desire to stay on top can blind him to reality, and he can self-destruct
- He can have an inflated ego and be power-driven
- He is cut off from his emotions and makes decisions from his head
- He feels entitled to have what he wants, including any woman he wants

Hera and Zeus:
Will They Live Happily Ever After?

O, two such silver currents, when they join
Do glorify the banks that bound them in.

– WILLIAM SHAKESPEARE, *KING JOHN*

The Zeus man and the Hera woman are about marriage – blissful marriage, successful marriage, working-at-it marriage, broken marriage, second or third marriage. When the two meet, they experience something between them that is bigger than physical attraction or falling in love. This bigger thing is the *heiros gamos,* the sacrament of marriage. It draws them together so they may fulfil its course. What pulls them together is not the sexual magnetism of Aphrodite and Ares or the love between soul mates of Artemis and Apollo. It's more a passion for the partnership and completion they feel in each other's presence. They are like a single coin with two sides, the feminine and the masculine. They meet as equals. He sees in her a strength and a dependability that he trusts can rise with him to life's pinnacle, and he makes her his queen. She knows that he will protect her and provide for her, and she will find wholeness as she steps forward to live in the fullness of her feminine power.

In the course of their marriage there will be circumstances that test their commitment to each other. As Joseph Campbell so beautifully writes in *The Power of Myth,* 'What is marriage? . . . It's the reunion of the separated duad. . . . It's different from a love affair. It's another mythological plane of experience. When people get married because they think it's a long-time love affair, they'll be divorced very soon, because all love affairs end in disappointment. But marriage is recognition of a spiritual identity. . . .

Marriage is not a simple love affair, it's an ordeal, and the ordeal is the sacrifice of the ego to a relationship in which two have become one'.

When a Hera/Zeus marriage is at its best, she becomes the centre of his world, and she makes him the centre of hers. He doesn't try to dominate her, and she doesn't try to control him. Both are holding the vision of what they are creating together. Although they might have great friendships outside the marriage, usually with same-sex friends, they always return to each other. If she is having a meeting with her girlfriends, she's going to make sure she's home when he returns. This is a relationship where there are no hidden thoughts. They know each other so well that they can often complete each other's sentences.

She is his calm in times of turmoil and provides for his every need. She is completely devoted to him, and his well-being is her priority. In *Candida* by Bernard Shaw, Candida says about her husband, James: 'I build a castle of comfort and love and indulgence for him, and stand sentinel always to keep little vulgar cares out. I make him master here, though he does not know it, and could not tell you a moment ago how it came to be so.' In this kind of relationship the husband and wife never take each other for granted. Their relationship is alive in and through the daily demands of life. There is no power struggle. They use their individual power to strengthen the union.

What makes this type of marriage work is that they strive to make each other's world better. She smoothes the edges for him. She knows his moods and whims and respects them. One woman said, 'If he comes home uptight about his day at work, I don't take it personally, and he never takes it out on me. I've learned to listen to him if he wants to talk, or to take his mind off it. We might just go have dinner, the two of us, or catch a movie. Or we go into our bedroom, and whether we have sex or not, just by lying together body and soul, he is comforted and I am recharged.' Her husband told me, 'I like the way she listens to me and doesn't tell me how to solve my problems. She's very present. And somehow, while she's listening, I find my own solutions.'

In the same way, another woman said to me, 'He constantly tells me he loves me. He compliments me and I feel his enjoyment of me in his life, and it makes me feel so cherished. If I want to get involved in the community, whether it be a charity or volunteering or taking a job, he never questions me but wholeheartedly supports me. He is my foundation.'

As Katherine says in Shakespeare's *The Taming of the Shrew:*

Thy husband is thy lord, thy life, thy keeper,
Thy head, thy sovereign; one that cares for thee,
And for thy maintenance commits his body
To painful labour both by sea and land,
To watch the night in storms, the day in cold,
Whilst thou liest warm at home, secure and safe;
And craves no other tribute at thy hands
But love, fair looks and true obedience;
Too little payment for so great a debt.

What draws Hera and Zeus together as partners is the desire to build a power base to create something larger, whether that be a family, a farm, a business, a new school or museum, or the mom-and-pop restaurant on the corner. Whatever it is, they join forces to bring forth an institution of some kind. They become society's pillars.

It is in aligning her efforts with those of her husband that the Hera woman finds and expresses her strength and power. If he is the sole breadwinner, she creates a home where he finds ease and can be restored. If he plows the fields and harvests the grain, she grinds the wheat and turns it into bread for their table. If he sets up a business arrangement, she creates the dinner party that charms the potential client and ultimately clinches the deal.

Their commitment to building something together transfers to their roles as parents. They raise their children to be part of what they're building, part of the family structure, the dynasty. They are likely to bring them up in a structured way, not encouraging a lot of independent thinking. They'll discuss the children's future together – what schools they go to, what friends they see, what time they come home. The children will be expected to abide by the family values. And if a child rebels against the father, the Hera mother will probably stand by her husband rather than her child, saying, 'This is what your father wishes.'

Every couple I've talked to who has a successful marriage says, 'We work at it.' For two to become one calls for a lot of sacrificing of ego, letting go of judgments, listening, communicating, cooperating and being creative in the relationship.

If they don't keep rekindling the relationship, their partnership can grow dull and routine, merely following the form of marriage. They might be giving more attention to what they're building – the store, the ranch, the family – and not enough to each other. He might become more involved at work while she is home alone or with the children too many evenings a week. She might slip into the archetypal pattern of the nagging wife, complaining about the kids or the house and criticising him for not spending enough time with the family. Or other archetypes might be pushing her to a less wifely, more independent role, and if she doesn't communicate her needs or he doesn't adjust, a rupture might arise in their relationship. Unless they are able to communicate openly with each other, the marriage is at risk. Or if he is not getting enough nurturing, attention and support at home or lovemaking, he will start having affairs to experience having his sexual power again. She will respond with mythic hurt, rage and jealousy. She might explode in fury and let him have it. Their home will become a battlefield. Or she might ask for a separation and then for a divorce, taking him for all she can. It is not uncommon for the marriage to go stale and for them to withdraw the energy and passion from each other. Not knowing how to rekindle the relationship and yet not wanting to leave, she might end up having an affair herself.

However, if their commitment to the partnership and to each other is solid, they will endure the hard times. When the bond is great enough, they will forgive each other. They will renew their marriage vows 'for richer or poorer'. This is the alchemy of marriage, where everything becomes grist for the mill. The frictions serve to purify the two personalities so the two souls can become one.

As Jacques Brel writes in 'Song of Old Lovers':

In spite of all we're still together
So many years of smiles and tears
How many times we'd part forever
And I would leave for parts unknown
A day a week and I'd feel terror
And crumble on the telephone
And then in bed we'd play confessions
And tell the truth what truth we knew

That's how it's been with me and you
And then we'd start upon a new digression

Oh my love
My old, my sweet, my gentle love
From year to year as all the seasons fall
I love you more, you know I love you

In spite of all we're still together
So many years of smiles and tears
How many times I found another
But you loved others too my dear
A day a week and I'd need a pardon
And fumble out the key for home
And take a wound that went unhealing
For you'd forgive without forgiving
But of course we went on living. . . .

And sometimes we were almost open
And sometimes we would almost touch. . . .

Oh my love
My old my sweet my gentle love
From year to year as all the seasons fall
I love you more, you know
I love you . . . still.

Elizabeth and Leonard:
Healing after the Affair

Elizabeth and Leonard are a prominent, successful New York couple. She is strong and confident, and very much her own person. He is intelligent, charming, authoritative and very clear about his goals. They met at a friend's home and, soon after, started dating.

He was keen to be married soon after they started the relationship. Although she felt the same pull to marry, she kept saying no. As a child, she had lived through her parents' unhappy marriage and subsequent divorce and felt the impact of her father's domineering personality. She found herself reluctant to surrender to risk such a situation again. Yet she loved Leonard and they kept seeing each other.

She describes the moment when she knew that she would marry him as transcendental. She met him at his office that Friday evening for a date, and they had another argument about getting married. There was a pause in the argument, and he stepped out to go to the bathroom. Suddenly she was hit by a strong sense of the future. She had a vision of what was to be, and she knew that this was the man she was going to marry. She said, 'It was as if God hit me on the head, and there was this deep, profound knowing.' Hera had spoken. When he returned, she told him, 'You are not going to believe this, but I am going to marry you.' He responded with a smile, 'Of course you are. I've always known that.'

They married and began building a happy life together. He was working his way up in the Manhattan marketing firm where he was employed. She was working at a non-profit organisation for cancer research. When she was pregnant with their first son, she gave up her work and turned her full attention to her marriage and family.

Seven years into the marriage, Leonard's ex-wife died of leukaemia, and his two sons from that marriage, aged fourteen and eight, came to live with them. They joined Leonard and Elizabeth's own sons, now eight and five, and suddenly they were raising a household of four boisterous boys.

Two years later, Leonard became president of his firm, just when the company went global. He was delighted to finally be able to guide the company according to his own vision, but he was also under tremendous pressure. By this time his oldest son had become a rebellious sixteen-year-old who was dangerous to himself and his family; he made daily threats to set the house on fire, kill someone or himself, missed school and got involved with drugs. Every day there was something, and Elizabeth lived in fear that the boy would one day carry out his threats. She worried about the effect on the younger boys, but she chose not to burden Leonard with the details. She wanted their home to be a place where he could come from work and not deal with more problems than those he was handling at the office. She thoroughly believed that was what a wife should do – endure the burdens at home so she can support what he does, which is to go out there and fight the battles at work and earn the money. However, the situation was taking its toll on their relationship. The situation became tense between them. He was becoming very irritable and she kept putting up with him.

On one of those tense mornings the phone rang, and Elizabeth picked it up. Leonard was getting dressed for work. The woman's voice on the other end – a voice she recognised as one of Leonard's colleagues at work, said, 'Hi, Elizabeth,' and asked for Leonard. On the phone he was abrupt and awkward. 'We'll talk about it when I am at the office. Yes, yes. . . . No, no I didn't. . . . We'll talk about it when I get to the office.' *Click.*

Elizabeth knew something was up. She sat down on the bed and looked at him. He looked directly at her and said, 'I am having an affair, and it's best that I move out today.'

She has never found the words to describe the surge of emotion of that moment. She went numb and speechless. The floor seemed to fall away under her feet. She watched him go out the door, and then fell on the bed and wept.

The next two years were horrible. He came and went. He didn't want a divorce, and amazingly, she found she didn't want one either. The children were one of their big concerns. He rented an apartment and sometimes spent the night there with the other woman, sometimes by himself, and sometimes at their home, sleeping in the guest bedroom. He was in tremendous pain, swept away by the force of passion yet full of guilt and remorse. He didn't know what he wanted. But he knew he didn't want to marry the other woman, and he knew he didn't want to leave Elizabeth and get a divorce. He still loved her.

She endured. At one point she met someone she liked and had an affair herself. And she found a very compassionate therapist.

Over time, Leonard started to come home more often, wanting to spend more time with her. She would refuse him. Finally, almost two years to the day he had left, he told her that the affair was over, and that he wanted to come back. She responded, 'The ship has sailed. We are done, done, done.' But he persisted. One day he showed up at their house at lunchtime and said, 'Let's make a deal. Take me back for seven days, and if in seven days you don't want me back, I'll leave you alone.'

She agreed to this offer. During those seven days she vented her heart out. She let him have it, calling him names, being meaner and nastier than she had ever known herself to be. He became the most tender, loving man and kept saying over and over, 'Elizabeth, I love you with all my heart and I never stopped loving you.' She commented later that his higher self seemed to have taken over. He was strong. He knew that he had wounded her and that the only way she could heal was if he allowed her to express her feelings and unconditionally loved her. She had to let her anger and pain out in whatever way she needed, and she needed to be loved. So he loved her in a most noble way by letting her be exactly how she wanted to be with him. He was majestic, she said. He was seeing the larger picture and was holding out for her healing and their being together. Like a true Zeus, he was being strategic, but his care and attentiveness were authentic.

He became the true benevolent king. He kept saying, 'Elizabeth, I love you with all my heart.' He must have said it a thousand times. He must have said it out loud, silently, and in his sleep. He never defended himself or tried to explain. On the contrary, he kept saying, 'You have every right to do this.' He asked nothing for himself, not even forgiveness. He was 100 percent present for her, letting her have all the space she needed to vent the anger and pain endured and suppressed all those months. It felt good to let it go. 'Finally,' she would think, 'he gets to experience some of the pain I have felt.' Seven days passed and she didn't kick him out. She liked this new permission to fully express her negative feelings and began to feel empowered.

One morning, six weeks into the 'suffering of Leonard', as she called it, after she had said something mean to him, he looked at her deeply, put his arms around her and said,

'Elizabeth, I think what we've been doing is no longer necessary and it is time we can end it, because I love you with all my heart.' She knew she was done. She fell in his arms and cried. All her fears and distrust just left her in that moment, and a healing of her heart took place. As he was leaving the house for work, she whispered, 'Thank God.'

She knew then how much she mattered to him. He had put up with all that because he truly loved her. This, she would say later, was the magic of how their relationship healed – he was prepared to go through anything to get her back. Then she remembered how she had known the future that day years earlier in his office, and, in the same way, she knew everything was going to be all right again. They have been in love ever since.

Now, thirty years later, they have a wonderful, fulfiling marriage, enjoying and loving each other, enjoying their grandchildren. They really are living happily ever after. When I asked Elizabeth if she and Leonard work at their marriage, she responded, 'I don't believe in working at it anymore. I did that. Now I just have a wonderful time being married. I love everything about him and I feel cherished. Sometimes I just ask myself, "How did I get so lucky?"'

Hera Speaks

I am Hera,
The feminine of hero,
And I am indeed a heroine,
Married beyond my will.
My brother Zeus became a cuckoo
And hid under my arms.
I took pity on him, of course I did,

That is my nature, noble and benevolent.
I was content and happy till he came and ravished me.
He implored me, begged me, seduced me into marry-
ing him
To become queen of Olympus,
To sit on the golden throne next to him.
My pride is well-known,
I succumbed to the glory of ruling.
Three hundred years we mated,
We gloried under the canopy of love.
Then his wantonness arose.
He mated nymphs, goddesses and mortals.
I bore him three children – Ares, Hephaestus and
Hebe.
He bore his own,
Birthing Athena out of his own head.
He humiliated and dishonoured me in every way he
could.
Our marriage was disavowed, my heart was broken.
I took revenge, my rage knew no end,
Till one day I left
And went home to Evia,
To live in solitude.
I took myself back intact,
And when I returned, I ruled in a whole new way
Because first I ruled myself.

Chapter 8

ATHENA, GODDESS OF WISDOM AND LEADERSHIP

The Athena Woman: Female Warrior

You have brains in your head.
You have feet in your shoes.
You can steer yourself any direction you choose.

— Dr Seuss

Athena is the smart, hardworking girl of Olympus. The minute she steps out of her father's head, fully grown and fully armed, she is ready for action. She guides the heroes she so loves and guards the city of Athens and its civilisation. She has a brilliant mind and the gift of oratory, and she can persuade others to follow their higher wisdom and judgment. She is aligned with the patriarchy of her father, Zeus, who favours her among all his children. He gives her ready access to his thunderbolts and lets her borrow his special shield, the aegis. However, she is a peaceful warrior. She uses her power astutely, for the good of all, not like her bloodthirsty brother Ares, who loves the frenzy of the battle-field. She joins the battle only to offer strategy to her favourite heroes and help them win, but she has nothing to do with the bloodshed of war. She is an expert negotiator, and as the goddess of weaving, she networks at Olympus.

The Athena woman embodies the goddess's mighty quali-ties here on earth. We marvel as we see her at a young age lost in her books, excelling at school, thirsting for knowledge and achieving at the highest level. She probably dislikes physical activities and would rather study science or maths or write her essays than play basketball or soccer. She leaves sports to her sister goddess Artemis. She doesn't care about her looks and doesn't spend hours dressing like Aphrodite. As she grows up she begins to notice boys, but she doesn't quite know what to do with them and they don't know what to do with her. So she makes them her friends and ends up discussing politics or social issues with them. She is the woman who thrives in any profession that uses her men-tal capabilities – law, medicine, science, journalism. She will put in the long hours to get her degree and then go to work and climb the career ladder.

My sister, Arianna Huffington, is an Athena. I used to watch how she was devoted to her studies from a young age, and when it came time to choose a university, she de-cided, with my mother's help, to go to Cambridge. She worked hard and got accepted. Just a few days after she ar-rived at the university, she heard about the debating society, Cambridge Union, and knew she wanted to be part of it. She threw herself into a field she knew nothing about. She had never debated before, but she found people who were good at it and then practised diligently. She took part in every debate and learned from her mistakes, becoming better and better with practice. She then decided to run for secretary of the union, a position that she won, and she eventually became president of the Cambridge Union Society, a very prestigious position. She was the third woman and the first foreign woman to ever win the honour. It opened many doors for her, the first of which was an offer to write her first book, *The Female Woman,* an immediate success. With her Athena discernment and focused vision she had chosen the path that would move her forward into her life's work.

The Athena woman thrives on her work. She works tirelessly and with consistent energy because she is not pulled by the unconscious dream world of Persephone or the romantic fantasies of Aphrodite. She is completely comfortable with her male colleagues, knowing she is as capable as they are. She is equally at home in leadership positions because she trusts her power and is not afraid to use it. We see her in every woman who has ever held a position of power in the world. A recent *Fortune* magazine featured the photographs of fifty powerful female CEOs, and in each one I saw the face of Athena.

We also see Athena in Cate Blanchett playing Queen Elizabeth I of England, daughter of Henry VIII, in the movie *Elizabeth.* We watch the young woman's Athena aspect take root and grow as she evolves into her role as queen. She says to one of her advisers, 'I may be a woman, Sir William, but if I choose, I have the heart of a man. I am my father's daughter, and I'm not afraid of anything.'

Elizabeth ruled England as the virgin queen, surrounded by devoted courtiers such as Sir Walter Raleigh and Sir Francis Drake. Similarly, in the myth, Athena has no lovers and stays a virgin, but she mentors many heroes. She helps Bellerophon capture Pegasus, the winged horse, and bridle him, which represents the power of ingenuity and skill over brute strength. She aids Perseus in safely slaying the snake-haired Gorgon Medusa, the direct sight of whom turns the viewer to stone. She gives him her polished shield so he can safely see the Gorgon as a reflection on its shiny surface. She guides Achilles in mastering his emotions when he is ready to slay his ally Agamemnon. And she helps her beloved Odysseus make it back home to Ithaca after years of adversities.

In the same way, the Athena woman easily becomes a great friend to men. She befriends men who are likely to succeed or who are already successful – she needs her heroes around her. Men take her out to dinner not to court her but to talk about their troubles at work or their relationships or their next step in life. She enjoys listening and offers counsel, coming up with crafty ideas to solve problems. After all, she is the one who helped the Greeks win the Trojan War by giving Odysseus the idea of the Trojan Horse.

She holds a large-scale vision and is able to sustain it over time and work steadily to see it to fruition. She is fearless about speaking out where injustice is done. A warrior for truth, she recognises when wrong is being done and takes the action necessary to fix it. People feel her strength and are drawn to her, for they want to be part of the social change she envisions. In the movie *Silkwood*, Meryl Streep portrays a courageous woman who spoke out against dangerous conditions at the nuclear processing plant where she was an employee. And in *Norma Rae*, Sally Field plays a cotton mill minimum-wage worker who became a firebrand rallying for better conditions for the employees. Feminist writer and activist Gloria Steinem has worked heroically for women's rights, shaping the feminist movement and contributing profoundly to the lives of millions of women.

When Anita Hill spoke out during the Senate hearings on Clarence Thomas's nomination to the Supreme Court that he had sexually harassed her, she raised awareness of women's rights in the workplace.

Award-winning CNN foreign correspondent Christiane Amanpour, who has reported on events from Bosnia, Somalia, and Israel to Afghanistan and Iraq, was once asked why she is willing to put her life at risk to cover the news. She responded, 'Because it matters, because the world will care once people see our stories, because if the storytellers don't do this, then the bad people will win. I believe that good journalism can make a difference in the world and that democracy depends on an informed citizenry. And so that's what keeps me committed to doing this job.'

As much as the Athena woman has confidence in her work, she lacks assurance in the love domain. She might date, but she often feels awkward, and when it comes to feelings and expressing them, she finds herself in a foreign land. In the myth, Zeus, Athena's father, swallows her mother, Metis. He suffers a splitting headache and he asks Prometheus to crack his head open, and that is how Athena is born. She never meets her mother; she is denied that nurturing and a connection with the feminine. In the Athena woman's psyche, this translates as her unexplored, feminine, vulnerable side, an aspect of herself that often terrifies her. She hides in her head and protects her heart behind her armoured breastplate. She is highly protective of herself because she doesn't like to feel out of control or powerless, especially when it comes to intimacy with a man. She needs to hold hands with her Demeter aspect, the one who can help her heal the absence of the mother principle she never had. This allows her to become softer, kinder and more receptive to life.

If she does not connect with this aspect of herself, she risks becoming cold, competitive, dismissive and condescending. She is threatened by emotionally available women, or by any expression of spontaneity and freedom. Such a woman can be a challenge to work with. In the myth, the maiden Arachne wove a tapestry so perfect that the goddess could not find fault with it. In anger, Athena turned the girl into a spider, condemning her to eternally spin works that would always be destroyed. This is the dark side of the Athena archetype. When a woman has this competitive Athena aspect, she will be reluctant to help other women up the ladder of success or open doors for them, even if she is in a position to do so.

The cold, intimidating Athena woman becomes like the Gorgon Medusa, whose head the goddess wore on her breastplate. In other words, her heart has turned to stone. She will bring down the life force of those around her, and they'll feel drained and fearful. This dark Medusa can have the same effect in the psyche of any woman who has not known nurturing. Just as she is about to develop a new idea or embark on a new project, the Medusa inside of her will say, 'You can't do that. Who do you think you are?' At which point she is filled with self-doubt and withdraws from what she had set out to do. At all costs, a woman has to address this internal voice and exorcise it out of her consciousness for inspiration and manifestation to breathe within her.

So many Athena women line up with their masculine, achievement-oriented side and sacrifice their feminine, nurturing side because the archetype directs them in this way. And since they are so successful at what they do, they might not be aware that they are missing something. As an Athena woman begins to inquire into this otherwise unknown side of herself – her inner maiden – she meets the caring, beautiful woman behind her keen mind and her remarkable achievements. She takes off her helmet, lets her hair down and stands tall in her magnificence, valuing herself for herself. She is reborn – this time getting out of her own head – and her life opens up to her heart and soul. She becomes twice as powerful as before. She can touch more people with her work because she is more accessible; her compassion is more obvious. She enjoys life more because her entire self is engaged – she is more aware, more alive, giving herself permission to have fun, to play, to savour life. This often happens when she falls in love.

The first time an Athena woman does something that is not written in her daybook or just for fun, she can feel the armour beginning to chip away. A friend of mine, the founder and busy CEO of a successful company, decided to sign up for a salsa dancing class on Tuesdays and began saying yes to spontaneous shopping trips with girlfriends. When she showed me the change in her closet – fewer grey suits and more colour and feminine clothes – I knew she was making room in her life for the sensual Aphrodite.

When it comes to her sexuality, an Athena woman can feel disconnected from her body because she lives so much in her head. She would do well to connect with the physicality of her Artemis aspect. If she is not married, she can go for long periods without even thinking about sex and feel fine without it. If she is married, she may regard sex simply as part of being a wife. She enjoys it up to a point, but she is not one to let physical passion take her over. One man was amused to find that, after intercourse, his Athena partner would always reach for her eyeglasses.

Falling in love can be a threatening experience for the Athena woman because she is asked to feel and to give up control. At the beginning she may deny that it is happening, but then she might gradually let down her guard. If she does open up and the man leaves her, she may shut right down again and not open up again for a long time, if ever. She'll throw herself into her work and pretend the vulnerable moment never happened.

For an Athena woman to open up to a man, he must be someone she respects. He must show her his vulnerability, which will make her feel safe enough to be vulnerable herself. Just as Athena encouraged her heroes, he might have to encourage her, reflecting back to her the beauty he sees. Then she can see herself, maybe for the first time, through the eyes of a man who loves her. She'll fall in love with herself and then with him. And then she just might forget about her glasses.

Her Strengths

- She has a clear, sharp mind and a keen wit
- She is a dependable and reliable ally to her partner
- She is a life force for mobilising change in society
- She cares for the good of all and is an asset in any organisation
- She is a great strategist and a peacemaker
- She is disciplined, focused, organised and works tirelessly to carry out her plans

Her Vulnerabilities

- She can become driven by her ambition to succeed and accomplish and neglect her soulful aspect

- She can be cut off from her emotions, her caring and be cold and aloof
- She can dismiss people if they don't meet her level
- She can be unable to let a man close to her emotions
- She can lack sensuality and femininity and be judgmental of the Aphrodite woman
- Her efficiency of organisation and planning can overrule any spontaneity and living in the moment

The Zeus Man Paired with Athena

Although in the myth Zeus is paired in marriage with Hera, he has another significant relationship with the goddess Athena. She is his cherished daughter, born out of his own head. His relationship with her brings out a side of him different from the one evoked by Hera – more intellectual, paternal and protective. Proud of his daughter's achievements, he allows her into his world in a way he would permit no other god or goddess. He gives her access to his thunderbolts and his special shield, the aegis, and thereby empowers her with his own strength. She, in turn, is proud to be Zeus's daughter. Never the rebellious child, she has Zeus's strengths – a far-reaching vision, comfort in wielding power, strategy in accomplishing her goals, craftiness in battle.

A Zeus man is often attracted to such a woman, one who can be his partner not because she complements and supports him, as a Hera woman does, but because she is so like him. This is not a sensual, erotic attraction, expressed in the myth as the god's pursuit after nymphs and maidens. Rather, it's a high-level, intellectual kind of partnership. He adores the way she embodies so many qualities like his own, but in feminine form. What could be more charming? This is a woman he can let into his life, to share his power and aspirations. He senses that she can climb to the top alongside him and be comfortable there by his side. In fact, she may have her own mountain peak, right alongside his.

A Zeus man suits the Athena woman as a mate, as well. She seeks a partner whom she admires and respects, someone who is confident, successful and is making his mark in the world. She expects the same high standards from her man that she expects from herself. Whereas with the young heroes she mentors Athena is always the senior, the older sister, and personal coach; in the Zeus man she sees someone who can match her level of accomplishment. She is attracted to his power and his ability to make things happen.

Athena and Zeus: Lifelong Equal Partners

A great part of all the pleasure of love begins, continues and sometimes ends with conversation. A real, enduring love-affair, in marriage and out of it, is an extremely exclusive club of which the entire membership is two co-equal perpetual presidents.

– ROBERTSON DAVIES, *THE PLEASURES OF LOVE*

When Henry Higgins exclaims in *My Fair Lady,* 'Why can't a woman be more like a man?' it's clear he has not yet met the Athena woman. If a man wants a partner who can match him in skills and practical thinking, let him seek out one of the Athenas of the world. Whereas the Hera woman is first a wife, the Athena woman is committed first to herself and then to being a wife. She has her own work and her own aspirations, and the marriage supports who she is.

In a thriving Athena/Zeus relationship, both partners

work, perhaps even in the same profession, and both con-tribute financially. The relationship succeeds because it's about two independent people who are not looking to each other to feel good about who they are. They know how to take care of themselves, they have their own goals and they are looking in the same direction. They bring the same com-mitment to their relationship as they do to everything else in their lives. These are not two people who will walk out at the first crisis. They are in it for the long haul, and they are going to make it work. They may be passionate about what they do, but they are not emotional, and that keeps their life together clear and uncomplicated. He is proud of her, and she loves having his protective presence in her life. One Athena/Zeus couple I spoke to told me, 'We are a mutual admiration society. We find that although we enjoy our friends, we don't really need anyone else. We're best friends. We converse about everything and never get bored with each other.'

The love between them is the archetypal love between fa-ther and daughter translated into the love of husband and wife. It is an eros of the mind, powerful and deep. It is not romantic fantasy, built on passing illusions, but a mature form of eros. It pulsates under the surface always – eros when they work, eros when they fight, eros when they are running their busy lives. Even if they don't feel it, it is pre-sent. He knows at some unconscious level that she is his; he birthed her and now she is her own person, and he loves her for that. So he takes her at night and makes love to her and feels complete and fulfiled; his world is never empty, no matter what. And when they make love, her feminine takes in his maleness and her masculine draws out his feminine, which she so loves. And with him by her side, life is rich. She knows she is loved, protected and safe, no matter what.

Shakespeare captured the essence of the Athena/Zeus couple when he wrote:

Let me not to the marriage of true minds
Admit impediments; love is not love
Which alters when it alteration finds,
Or bends with the remover to remove.
O, no, it is an ever-fixed mark
That looks on tempest and is never shaken.

In the movie *Adam's Rib,* starring Katharine Hepburn and Spencer Tracy, we see the archetypal relationship of Athena and Zeus in full bloom. They are two lawyers, Amanda and Adam, married, in love and fully involved in the daily rituals of a romantic relationship, laced with intellectual repartee – breakfast and reading the morning paper in bed, and after a day of legal cases enjoying each other's company with the usual drink and making dinner together. However, their relationship is put to the test when they end up representing opposing sides in a court case between a wife and husband. Amanda takes on the wife's case, outraged that the woman might be convicted of assaulting her husband while he gets away with abusing and cheating on her, and she wins in court – though her Athena assertiveness and strategising push her own marriage to the brink of divorce. Adam softens, however, when he realises how much they have together, and their relationship weaves back together again. They know the eros between them is unbreakable.

If an Athena/Zeus couple is raising a family, they will look to their children's well-being on a large scale. They give high priority to preparing them for the world, guiding them toward a college education and eventual career, and keeping an eye on the company they keep. They will take them to museums, to concerts and sports events, and if they're not doing well at school, will find them a tutor. The Athena mom will not give up her career for her children, but she will strategise and juggle schedules to make it all work. She may coach and guide her sons and daughters just as the goddess mentored her ancient Greek heroes, encouraging and supporting them, and telling them they can achieve what they set out to do.

The shadow aspect of the Athena archetype may show up as a competitive streak, which can slip into the Athena woman's relationship with her mate in numerous ways. If they are at dinner with friends, she finds ways to show off how smart and informed she is. If they are driving, she knows the best route. If they are buying a house, she can find the best deal. She tries to score one up on everything. It may be unconscious on her part, and if you point it out to her, she defends herself, saying she is only acting on what she knows is right. Or she may become bossy and controlling, in which case the Zeus ego is not going to like it at all. He will fight back, and their relationship may become a battleground between two crafty warriors of the mind – arguing, disproving each other's points, engaging in verbal one-upmanship. The stage play and movie, *The Lion in Winter*, portrays the famous relationship between Henry II of England and his wife, Eleanor of Aquitaine. They are known through the centuries for their competitiveness and bickering, and the stakes were high. The successor to the throne of England and vast territories of France hung in the balance.

The shadow of the Zeus archetype is his appetite for seducing women, and if this shows up in the context of a marriage, the Zeus man may find himself in an extramarital affair. When his Athena partner discovers this, she will be devastated, but she will endure and put up a front. She holds the larger picture of the marriage. When Bill Clinton's encounter with Monica Lewinsky became public, Hillary Clinton summoned up her personal strength, ignored public opinion and moved on with her purpose, eventually seizing an opportunity to become a U.S. senator. The Athena woman may be wounded, and the relationship may suffer, but she moves on with her life – and the relationship may survive as well.

Another difficulty the Zeus man faces is his inability to admit any kind of weakness or defeat. If things at work are not going according to plan, he may put on a show of bravado, pretending that everything is all right and telling himself he still has a few tricks up his sleeve. The smart Athena woman probably intuits the situation. She needs to evoke her Hestia presence, coming less from her intellect and more from her heart, and create a safe place where he can tell her what's going on and not feel that she will withdraw her love or be critical.

Both of them run the danger of their lives becoming increasingly success-driven, filled with work and family, and running on automatic. They may lose touch entirely with the eros that fuels their relationship – too tired at the end of the day to share experiences, to talk things over, or make love. They can go on in this way for a while – or for the duration of their lives – but they're running on empty, and after a while the emptiness of a life that is strictly about achievements takes its toll.

Hopefully, one of them will remember the larger picture, and then they can turn their gifts for problem solving to their relationship. They can set in motion a new intention for their relationship – more quality time together, more loving, more humour. I knew a model Athena/Zeus couple like that. It wasn't until he had a heart attack that they heard the wake-up call. She told me she tried to go to work the next day, but in the wake of her husband's life-threatening crisis her priorities had shifted. 'It was the first time in my life that I couldn't concentrate, I couldn't focus. I had to go be with him and do something meaningful.' When he recovered, they made an agreement that Sundays would be a day just for them. No phones, no social activities. They would spend the day together, rejuvenating themselves and their relationship – reading, listening to music, taking walks in the park, preparing a leisurely meal – a true day of rest.

The Athena and Zeus archetypes are the Olympian heavyweights who know how to deal with adversities. When such a couple applies their skills and gifts to their own relationship, they have a good chance of success. Eleanor Roosevelt, after thirteen years of marriage and six children, suffered the shock of discovering that her husband, Franklin, was involved with another woman. 'The bottom dropped out of my own particular world,' she said later. 'I faced myself, my surroundings, my world honestly for the first time.' There was talk of divorce, but Franklin promised not to see the woman again, and the idea was dropped.

From this time forward, however, Eleanor no longer defined herself in terms of her husband's wants and needs. There was a new relationship between them. She gradually stepped forward into her role as a powerful voice for social change. When Franklin was paralysed with polio, she became his eyes and ears, travelling, speaking and meeting people when he could not. She lined up behind him body, mind and soul to help him become president of the United States. She saw the vision of what they could do together for the country. Once he was elected, she transformed the role of First Lady into first lady for the people, using it as a platform to work ceaselessly yet with characteristic grace for humanitarian issues and social justice. It is said that when Franklin went to bed at night he would pray, 'Please, God, make Eleanor tired'. In the Roosevelts' life and work we see the impact that the Athena and Zeus archetypes together can make on society. The husband and wife living under these archetypes share their lives and their gifts, and bring the fruits of their gifts to society.

Joan and David: Outlasting Life's Challenges

They met while on vacation at a health resort and hit it off right away. David was a Silicon Valley venture capitalist, and Joan worked for a San Francisco advertising agency. He was forty-four, divorced and had two sons; she was thirteen years his junior, divorced as well, but had no children.

Joan was dating someone else when she met David, but it wasn't a serious relationship and she ended it not long after. 'I was attracted to David's intelligence. He seemed larger than life, vibrant and interested in so many things, and he was witty and charming. He exuded power, but I could see that underneath he was vulnerable and gentle. He wasn't macho, and clearly he adored women.' David was attracted to her physically and appreciated her fine mind, and he could see in her eyes that she enjoyed being with him.

After they had been dating about a year, David wanted to get married, but Joan was happy the way things were. After all, they were in a committed relationship. To her it didn't matter whether they signed the legal papers or if she wore a ring on her finger. But when she realised how important it was to him, she agreed.

When I asked her if they were in love, Joan told me that it wasn't the heady excitement of infatuation. The love she felt for him was different from any she had known before. It was solid and real. It felt like they were meant to be together. There was a high level of comfort and honesty between them – absolutely no pretence. They had a lot in common, though they differed in the way they did things – she was more practical and he was more 'let's live in the moment'. He was generous with her and was happy to let her be her own person. She was happy that he completely accepted her family and friends. They had many good times together. However, they were both strong personalities with their own views, and there was often friction between them. She left her job when they got married and joined his company, an experience she described as both exhilarating and frustrating since they wanted to do things differently, and of course each of them thought they were right. They argued quite a bit – to the point where one day one of Joan's friends quipped, 'You two need a car with two steering wheels.'

Ten years into the marriage, the downward turn in the dot.com business took its toll on David's company. Businesses kept folding one after the other. Although David was optimistic and cavalier about it, the financial reality began to hit home. Accustomed to being in control and making things happen, David never stopped working hard or believing that the next opportunity was around the corner, but after two years of possibilities that never made it, their boat was clearly being rocked.

Joan could see the writing on the wall. She didn't blame David, because she knew how hard he was trying. Her Athena ability to clearly assess the situation came forth, and she decided to step in and take action. She told David she would look for work outside their company, and he supported and encouraged her. Joan knew she could find the kind of position she wanted, and she started calling former colleagues to say she was looking. One day the phone rang. A prominent East Coast advertising firm was opening a new global division in New York City, and they were offering her a position as vice president. New York City – it was three thousand miles away, but the job would bring in enough to support her in New York and keep them both afloat. It was also a great career opportunity for Joan. She was about to become their primary breadwinner – a switch of roles after twelve years of marriage.

A Hera woman would never think of leaving her husband and going to another city, however much the boat was at risk of going under, but an Athena woman will do what it takes to solve the problem. Two months later, Joan moved to New York and started a new life. It was difficult at first. She was alone, and she missed David and her home and her friends. For the first few months she cried herself to sleep every night, and when David came to know of it, he said she should come back to San Francisco, that they would make it somehow. She knew, however, that going back was not the answer and that she would see herself through the adjustment period. David came to New York every other weekend to spend time with her.

Joan told me, 'I never thought of leaving the marriage; that was never an issue. No matter how hard things get, I never quit. I don't believe in quitting. I am in it for the distance. When I married David, it was for life. If you stick together, you'll get through it, one day at a time.' Then she added, with the inimitable pragmatic wisdom of an Athena woman: 'Love is a cyclical thing. You fall in love, you fall out of love, you dislike the person, then you want to kill them, you can't believe you are with them – and then you love them again. You don't have to love them every day. Love goes through seasons like everything else. No human being can love another every day, and I am okay with that. I just deal with the stuff of the day as it presents itself.'

Joan and David have been living on opposite coasts for two years now. She has made a life for herself in New York and is very successful. His company has started to put some deals together again. He still travels to New York twice a month, and she comes to San Francisco whenever she can. He has also faced and come through a major illness. Their commitment to each other has sustained them through the challenging chapters of their life as a couple. 'At the end of the day,' she says, 'we are in it together, and we'll face everything together.'

She is contemplating making the move back to San Francisco. And one of these days she might get that car with two steering wheels – or maybe she'll make one.

Athena Speaks

Come into my temple of wisdom,
Where your thoughts are clear
And your heart is brave.
I'll come with you into the battlefield,
And you will win.
I'll show you how to triumph
Where proud men take up arms.
I know a wiser way,
So your victory will be sweet.
My mercy and soulful guidance
Are always with you.
You'll know your power, your centre.
You'll be shielded and protected.
My sword of truth will cut the way

So you'll know your way back home.
I brought Ulysses back to Ithaca,
Whispering in his ear
Words of courage and support,
So he never lost sight of the light
Even in the darkest hours.
Bright-eyed Athena they call me.
Embrace me, and you'll have dominion over your
    thoughts,
And with your bright brilliant mind and strength
You'll have the ear of all men.
I'll weave you a map of the world
And you'll know the pitfalls
Where not to go,
So you'll travel always safe.
Life with me is the art of
Weaving all things together
For the good of all.
The time has come.
You are needed in the world.
Come, follow me,
I'll be your inspiration.
I'll lead you to the all-knowing spirit
Which dwells in you.

Chapter 9

DEMETER, GODDESS OF THE EARTH

The Demeter Woman: Nurturing Mother

*In the beginning, people prayed to the Creatress of life,
the Mistress of Heaven. At the very dawn of religion,
God was woman. Do you remember?*

– MERLIN STONE, *WHEN GOD WAS A WOMAN*

The Demeter woman's heart beats with the desire to give life. Nurturing, generous, all-embracing, she finds her greatest fulfilment in giving birth, becoming a mother and raising her children. When you ask what work she does, she says, 'I am a mother,' with pride and dignity. Though these days society gives higher status to the woman who has a career, the Demeter woman knows mothering as the most honourable occupation for a woman and the greatest contribution she can make to society.

I will always remember a woman attendee at one of my workshops who so exquisitely embodied the Demeter archetype. Her face glowed as she held her infant daughter in her arms, breast-feeding her, while her three-year-old was at home being looked after by her own mother. The woman's main issue was that her husband didn't want any more children because of the financial responsibility. She was distraught that she might have to stop at two. She felt she had come to this earth with the sole mission of raising children.

Demeter, goddess of fertility and the harvest, was one of the most senior goddesses on Olympus, a sister of Zeus, Poseidon and Hera. Her mother, Rhea, was the ancient goddess of the earth, and her grandmother, Gaia, was the earth itself. As goddess of productivity and nurturing, she taught humankind to grow grain. While Athena produces in order to achieve a goal, Demeter produces in order to feed. The cornucopia is Demeter's symbol. She is a great archetype to call forth into our consciousness because she knows no lack. The earth is abundant, and so is she.

We look at the faces of women who have gone through catastrophes, who have lost their houses, their children, their husbands to war – women who have survived atrocities in Iraq, Afghanistan, Somalia, Bosnia – and we wonder how they endure. Their strength comes from knowing they are connected to the source of life, to the strength of the earth herself, and she sustains them. They love with the purpose of nurturing life, and they go on, regardless.

When she is angered, Demeter has the power to shake the roots of Mount Olympus. When Hades abducted her daughter, Persephone, with Zeus's consent, Demeter dressed herself in mourning and wandered the earth for days, searching for her child. In her grief and fury she threatened to let every growing thing dry up and die and so bring devastation to the earth. Zeus was forced to yield and bring Persephone back. There is nothing fiercer than a mother roused to protect her child.

My mother, Elli, was the embodiment of Demeter, magnificent and earthy. Everyone called her 'earth mother'. Once her two daughters were born, she gave herself over completely to raising them and caring for their every need. This gift of nurturing she extended to my father, too, and she looked to him to be the family man, but he still wanted to be the free Zeus and wanted things his way. Eventually my father began to seek mistresses and various forms of entertainment. This is one pattern that can accompany the Demeter woman: Once she becomes a mother, her attention shifts to her children, and unless her husband joins her in creating the family structure, he can feel left out – and he is. He will look elsewhere to get his needs met, and the marriage will suffer. Once my mother decided to separate from my father and raise us on her own, she shut herself off from men and, like the goddess, never had another relationship. However, we were never away from her except when we spent time with my father.

Elli was so in tune with our individual needs. My sister excelled in school, while I flourished in any form of artistic expression. My mother wanted to make sure my gifts were nurtured, not suppressed by the demands of school, so she continuously encouraged me and nurtured my interests in acting and dance. She made miracles happen in our lives. Just like the goddess, who created havoc on Olympus to get her daughter back, she did whatever it took to bring us the opportunities we needed. When my sister was preparing to go to the University of Cambridge, my mother arranged for the best tutor. When I was getting ready to go to the Royal Academy of Dramatic Arts in London, she found the perfect teacher to train me. Throughout our years in England she was with us, meeting our friends, guiding us in making the right decisions, and encouraging us to keep a positive outlook. She taught me more about life than anyone else by showing me how to keep a positive outlook and not waste my energy. She would say, 'Remember that you are your own capital. Invest in yourself.'

She fed everyone who came to our house, and this did not change when we moved to the United States. She was known for making sure that even the Federal Express man had a snack in his hand as he left our door. In her eyes, every person was worth connecting with. Whether she met you at the supermarket or at a black-tie dinner, it was with the same openness and genuine interest. Money, status and celebrity carried no influence with her. She cared about the authentic person. She believed that the moment of connecting with another was a true communion and was dismayed when people interacted with half their attention. She believed in being fully present in the moment. She used to tell me, 'If you want to be successful, give your full attention to what you are doing. Don't be fragmented.' Eating for her was another kind of communion. She abhorred the American idea of fast food. There should be nothing fast about food, she used to say. Food was a sacred ritual of life.

Going to the supermarket with her was a full morning's outing. If you weren't prepared to have a leisurely, fun-filled experience, it was better not to go along. The supermarket was her kingdom. She delighted in the abundance of fruits and vegetables and would buy cookies and candies and give them away to the children she met. She found such joy in this spontaneous expression of affection, and her aliveness was contagious. It pulled you into the moment. When it rained, she loved to walk barefoot on the earth. She was so in tune with the elements. She would say, 'Blessing, blessing, enjoy this blessing,' as if she could feel the earth's happiness in being watered.

She never rushed, or did things in a hectic way. She listened to her own rhythm and used to say, 'I have a rhythm of eternity.' When my sister and I were anxious about boyfriends or work or making a decision, she would wisely tell us, 'Let it marinate.' In that phrase was her whole philosophy. She knew that human consciousness is a laboratory where thoughts and feelings are steeped and mingled until they develop full flavour and ripen into a decision.

One evening when we were having dinner at a restaurant with friends, she casually asked the waiter what time it was. He said he didn't know because he didn't have a watch. She said, 'Would you like one?' 'Sure,' he replied, 'but I can't afford the one I want.' She happened to have my father's expensive French watch in her bag, which he had given her years earlier. She took it out and handed it to him and said, 'Now you have a watch, and a very good one.' He was speechless. Tears came to his eyes. She said, to all of us, 'Don't miss the chance to make another human being happy when life offers you the opportunity.' On a similar occasion, a woman admired her pearl necklace and she simply took it off and gave it to her. Stunned, the woman blurted out, 'What may I give you?' 'Nothing, my dear,' she responded. 'This is not a trade or an exchange. It is an offering.'

I always wished one thing for her: I wanted to see her receive more love and affection from the man she loved, my father. The times I saw my father give her that kind of attention, she would become more the woman and less the mother, and those were always happy moments for me. However, she found her heart's fulfilment in living the Demeter archetype, but living it fully required her to sacrifice other parts of herself so she would have no distractions. She was convinced that she couldn't give 100 per cent to her children if she was in a relationship. Her capacity to care was extraordinary, and her caring was always made tangible in action.

The night she died she was sitting on a chair, all of us gathered around her. She had had a stroke and knew it but had whispered to the housekeeper not to tell us. She insisted that we have something to eat and open a bottle of wine. We were sharing stories and laughing. She was fully present, listening to Greek music and singing. Then she gently passed away. Her memorial was like a feast, a celebration of life. She had asked that there be an abundance of chocolates and candies to give to the children. Family and many friends were there, as well as many taxi drivers, gardeners, postmen and Federal Express deliverymen.

I feel her huge spirit always present with me.

When you are around a Demeter woman, you feel embraced by love, warmed and welcomed. We love being around such women because all of us need to be loved in an unconditional way. Her maternal nature carries a spark of the divine. When this archetype is awakened in us even a little, it connects us to life and makes us not afraid. Fear comes from anticipating loss, from not having our needs met, but maternal love comes from the source where life is born. This nurturing mother is needed in us, around us, in our families and in society, to heal and to guide.

We see the Demeter woman as a young girl mothering her dolls, caring for younger siblings and classmates. As she grows up she becomes highly attuned to other people's feelings. If she chooses a profession, it will be one that puts her nurturing qualities to use – a nurse, a teacher, a masseuse, a caterer, a pediatrician. If she doesn't have children of her own, a career that calls on her archetypal nature can give her the opportunity to express her mothering genius. Oprah Winfrey is a great example of an archetypal Demeter. She nourishes people with ideas and encourages them to take care of and love themselves. Her television show focuses on enriching people's lives and serving the human spirit.

Being so responsive to other people's needs, it is easy for the Demeter woman to assume she has to help and support everyone. She can quickly lose her personal boundaries. She tends to put herself last. She very likely doesn't spend a lot of time on herself, dressing for comfort and practicality rather than to enhance her femininity. And it can be difficult for her to say no. If she is single, she might have a hard time saying no to the guy who likes her and wants to sleep with her because she doesn't want to hurt his feelings. If she becomes pregnant and then has to decide whether to go through with the pregnancy or not, she will have a hard time considering an abortion because her Demeter nature will want to keep and protect the child. And if she does have an abortion, she will go through a period of depression and grieving.

If she continues to take on more than she needs to or more than her capacity, she may begin to feel enslaved. She is giving, but it comes from a place of martyrdom instead of from the archetype's mythic abundance. She becomes depleted and exhausted. This inner pressure to be the super-mom to everything and everyone is exquisitely described by one mother in a *Redbook* magazine article: 'I wash the dishes, rush the older children off to school, dash out in the yard to cultivate the chrysanthemums, run back in to make a phone call about a committee meeting, help my youngest child build a block-house, spend fifteen minutes skimming the newspapers so I can be well informed, then scamper down to the washing machine where my thrice-weekly laundry includes enough clothes to keep a primitive village going for an entire year. By noon I'm ready for a padded cell.'

Because she has used herself up psychologically and emotionally, her body may try to make up for it by gaining weight. Gaining weight can also be an unconscious way to try to establish a more substantial boundary between herself and others. If a woman becomes conscious of this pattern and decides to break it, she needs a support system. It may be time for her to draw the line, ask for help and receive support and loving, perhaps from the very family members, friends and colleagues to whom she has been giving so generously. She may discover that she can let other people handle what is theirs to handle, even if they don't do it the same way or as well as she would.

When the Demeter woman looks for a partner, she seeks the man who will be the father of her children more than she seeks a husband for herself. The goddess Demeter mated with Zeus and from that union birthed Persephone; after that, she had very little to do with him. Similarly, once the Demeter woman has children, sex may hold less interest for her. She may value it more as the act of procreation and not necessarily as a pleasure in itself. She may be comfortable with just cuddling, which can become a problem in her marriage. Her maternal qualities might attract an immature man, one who is narcissistic and needs to be taken care of. Because of her readiness to be needed, she might marry him and then pay the price – she may find herself mothering both her children and her husband, who is not living up to his role as father and provider. As she finds a mate, she needs to call on the discernment of her Athena aspects to see if the man in her life is one who will be happy building a family with her.

The woman living under the Demeter archetype can suffer depression when her children grow up and leave home. Her life suddenly loses its purpose. This is a woman who needs a new direction. She has served the archetype as a mother, now she must let it guide her to find new people and situations to care for. So many women have used this moment of transition creatively and found a new purpose in life, starting new careers, volunteering where their help is needed, taking up an art form, or perhaps getting involved in social or political causes. This is an opportunity for a woman to expand the role of mother to nurture and give life to institutions, society and the needy. In the process, she will discover how profound her gifts are.

And she must do one more important thing: She must include herself in her giving. She must receive from the same source that she gives from and fill her own cup. When she is full, she gives out of her own abundance. Then she truly embodies the mother goddess, who is always full. She becomes her own cornucopia and can feast at her own banquet table along with others.

Her Strengths

- She is a caring, protective and nurturing partner
- She is a good listener – affectionate and compassionate
- No matter what project she undertakes, she brings in her caring and nurturing
- Her giving is bountiful, generous and inclusive
- She is a devoted and loving mother
- She has an affinity with nature and the earth

Her Vulnerabilities

- She can neglect herself and become depleted and exhausted
- She tends to feel overburdened and sorry for herself
- She can take too much responsibility for meeting other people's needs
- She can become a mother to her partner and lose sexual interest
- She can be overly protective and have difficulty letting go of her children
- If she is not nurturing herself psychologically, she will try to do it with food

The Poseidon Man: Full-Spectrum Passion

I hold a beast, an angel, and a madman in me, and my
enquiry is as to their working, and my problem is their
subjugation and victory, downthrow and upheaval,
and my effort is their self-expression.

– DYLAN THOMAS

In the centre of the Archaeological Museum in Athens stands the famous bronze statue of Poseidon, god of the sea. He stands with legs astride, arms raised, holding his trident, conveying the power of a god who can generate earthquakes and tidal waves. He commands the attention of the onlooker; you know immediately that this god is a force of nature, primal, elemental.

When Zeus, Hades and Poseidon divided the cosmos between them after defeating the Titans, Poseidon was given dominion over the oceans. He rules the turbulent seas, the source of all life, with his trident, a symbol of his sexuality. How often have we stood before the vast blue of the ocean, wondering on its mysteries. In the human psyche, Poseidon's realm is the emotional world with its massive waves of feeling and its bottomless depths, the world of the fluid unconscious.

If we could peek into the inner world of the Poseidon man, we would see a world much like the ocean – teeming with life, deep, and passionate. Hidden there is the soul of a man who feels intensely all the shades of the emotional life – he could be a poet, an artist, a musician. He embodies the big life force of the god Poseidon, a primordial, instinctive sexuality, and a yearning to give expression to his passions.

The journey of the Poseidon man can be solitary, for he is often not appreciated in our society, where success is measured in terms of materiality. He will suffer if he has to take a job just because it provides a paycheck, and it doesn't allow expression of his rich creative nature. If he gets entangled in the business world, he feels like a misfit and can be crushed. He lacks the strategies of his brother Zeus and often reacts emotionally in negotiations. He tends to be vengeful and can be a sour loser. In the *Odyssey*, Poseidon is the one who tosses challenge after challenge in Odysseus's path and causes his journey to last a decade because Odysseus has blinded Poseidon's son, the one-eyed monster Cyclops.

If the current of the Poseidon psyche is channelled properly, however, he can become a great therapist, like Carl Jung, exploring the depths of the unconscious, guiding others there, and gracefully pulling them up again. Or he may choose to dive into his own inner world where he can access humanity's collective depths and bring those depths to light through words, as did Ernest Hemingway, D. H. Lawrence,

Dylan Thomas, or Norman Mailer. Or, like van Gogh or Beethoven, he may express his powerful emotions in art or music. As an actor he brings emotional depth, passion and poetic strength to the roles he plays; consider the performances of actors such as Richard Burton, George C. Scott and Russell Crowe. As a director, such as Steven Spielberg, he can take us to worlds we cannot access on our own. Or he may plumb the deepest reaches of emotional and cultural patterning and explore the realm of myth, as did mythologist Joseph Campbell.

The bull and the stallion are associated with Poseidon and embody the essence of the archetype. Like the emotions, they are never fully under control; they are domesticated yet unpredictable, potent and virile. It takes skill and attention to work with them. The horse in particular has long been associated with the unconscious and with sexuality. Poseidon takes the form of a stallion when he takes advantage of the goddess Demeter. She plunges into the sea in search of her lost daughter, Persephone. He lusts after her, and paying no attention to her state of grief and distress, he pursues her. She transforms herself into a mare to avoid him, but he turns himself into a stallion and ravishes her.

Poseidon was truly in love with the sea nymph Amphitrite and wanted her to be his wife. He courted her and raped her. She was terrified and hid where she would be safe. Grief-stricken that he had lost his true love, he sent a dolphin to find her and bring her back. She did become his wife, and bore him three sons.

If the Poseidon man is frustrated in his creativity, he may try to fulfil the creative part of himself through a woman. Consumed by his world and his feelings, he can be blinded to what the person right in front of him is feeling or experiencing. Like the ocean itself, he is no respecter of boundaries.

This is the kind of man who cannot take no for an answer once he starts to make out with a woman, and she might suddenly find she has awakened a sleeping bull who might take her by force. And if the woman rejects him, he can sink into an abyss. To court and win the heart of the woman he loves, the Poseidon man must express his more imaginative, magical aspect, just as the god finally sent a playful, soulful intelligent dolphin to invite Amphitrite to come willingly to his side.

I remember working with a Poseidon-like man on a television project. I was captivated by his mysterious, deep way of expressing himself, and I loved working with him. We felt a mutual attraction. He was an Irishman, six feet two, and in that uniquely Irish way he was intense about everything. He talked endlessly about life, and philosophised and recited poetry to me as he sipped his whisky. He was a gifted writer, but as skilful as he was at evoking beautiful words, he had no skill in listening to a voice other than his own. He was a Poseidon man riding his own wave, and I knew if I got involved with him I would be pulled under that wave and get lost in the abyss. It took immense Athena discipline on my part not to give in to his seductive masculine emotionality, but I could see the consequences.

If he is lost in the world of his emotions, the Poseidon man will feel disconnected from others and, like a ship without a captain, let the winds take him where they will. He can get caught in a downward spiral of negative feelings about himself and then not accomplish anything and feel defeated. He might try to drown his emotions in drugs or alcohol and find himself caught even deeper in his turbulent psyche. He is capable of rage and becoming quarrelsome and vindictive. He can be the classic abusive drunk father, whose family has to endure his uncontrolled and dangerous torrent of emotions. If he doesn't manage his emotions, he'll sink, and the people around him will suffer. Afraid of his power, they are paralysed and feel incapable of taking action.

When Minos became king of Crete, Poseidon sent him a beautiful white bull as a sign of his favour. Minos was expected to sacrifice the bull to Poseidon, but the bull was so handsome that he didn't want to kill it. Enraged, Poseidon took revenge. He caused Minos's queen, Pasiphaë, to fall in love with the bull, and the fruit of their union was the Minotaur, the half-human, half-bull creature who lived in the famous labyrinth on Crete. The Minotaur became unmanageably wild, and finally Theseus, king of Athens, killed it. The Minotaur represents the half-tame, half-wild forces that the Poseidon man knows are part of him. Every bullfighter knows not to confront the bull head-on; only by using skill, timing and the deft movement of the flowing cape can he control the animal. Similarly, the Poseidon man must learn to tame his wild, bull-like nature.

Homer's *Odyssey* tells the story of Odysseus's ten-year journey home from Troy to Ithaca, struggling against the sea and the whims of the god Poseidon. His story is none other than the story of any man's struggle with his own dark side, the forces and patterns that lie in the depths of his psyche. His angry nature, his erratic behaviour, his self-destructive side are some of the aspects the man must confront and conquer, like Odysseus did, if he wants to come home to himself. In his famous poem *Ithaka*, the Greek poet Kavafi acknowledges the profundity of this journey:

As you set out for Ithaka
ask that your road be long,
full of adventure and instruction. . . .
The Laistrygonians and the Cyclops,

the angry Poseidon – fear them not.
You won't encounter them
unless you bring them along inside your soul,
unless your soul sets them up in front of you.

How should the Poseidon man proceed? By taking dominion of his erratic emotional patterns and developing some of the attributes of his other archetypes. Odysseus couldn't have made it without Athena's support, encouragement and guidance. The Poseidon man needs to call on the balanced wisdom of Athena, perhaps in the form of a woman therapist or a woman friend he bonds with. He also needs to access Apollo's rational thinking. And he must develop his Hermes aspect, harnessing those rich emotions, communicating them and giving them expression in art and creativity. Hephaestus, too, knew how to transmute his volcanic emotions into the making of beautiful things. Physical activities like martial arts can centre him and at the same time provide an outlet for his energies. A sport like golf can ground him and help him connect his body, mind and unconscious. It is important for him to take up a creative activity of some kind to bring his inner world into outer form.

The Poseidon man may have a natural affinity with the sea or with any body of water because it matches his own fluid nature. He may even take up sailing or kayaking as a hobby. He feels at home near the water. There, away from world's hustle and bustle, his emotions calm and he can think more clearly.

In *Memories, Dreams, Reflections,* Carl Jung talks about the transformation and deep communion with life he found at the house he built by a lake at Zurich, a place where he could find spiritual solace: 'At times I feel as if I am spread out over the landscape and inside things, and am myself living in every tree, in the splashing of the waves, in the clouds and in the animals that come and go, in the procession of the seasons. There is . . . nothing with which I am not linked. Here everything has its history and mine; here is space for the spaceless kingdom of the world's and the psyche's hinterland. Silence surrounds me almost audibly and I live "in modest harmony with nature" . . . here the torment of creation is lessened, creativity and play are close together.'

Just as Poseidon fell in love with a beautiful young man called Pelop, Oscar Wilde had a famous relationship with the young Lord Alfred Douglas. In Wilde's essay *De Profundis*, written to Douglas from prison, we hear the depths of the Poseidon soul searching for and finding the truth underneath things. 'Still, I am conscious now that behind all the Beauty, satisfying though it be, there is some Spirit hidden of which the painted forms and shapes are but modes of manifestation, and it is with this spirit that I desire to become in harmony. I have grown tired of the articulate utterances of men and things. The Mystical in Art, the Mystical in Life, the Mystical in Nature – this is what I am looking for, and in that great symphonies of Music, in that initiation of Sorrow, in the depths of the Sea I may find it. It is absolutely necessary for me to find it somewhere.'

Ultimately, the pull that the Poseidon man feels is the mystic's call to come home to the depths of his soul. Having ridden the currents of his passions and tamed his turbulent nature, he brings himself to shore. Kavafi beautifully describes the arrival of the Poseidon man at his true home:

> Have Ithaka always in your mind.
> Arriving there is what you're destined for.
> But don't in the least hurry the journey.
> Better if it lasts for years,

So when you arrive there you're old,
Rich with all you've gained on the way. . . .
So wise have you become, of such experience
That you must have understood by now what these
Ithakas are all about.

His Strengths

- He is a highly creative and stimulating partner to be with
- He feels his emotions deeply
- He is a passionate and sexual lover and thoroughly enjoys lovemaking
- He can draw on the depths of his feelings and produce great works of art
- If he wants you, he will move earth and sky to get you

His Vulnerabilities

- He can be angry and unable to control his emotions
- If he doesn't find creative outlets, he will suffer from low self-esteem and feel defeated
- He can be domineering and push himself on a woman when he wants her
- He is temperamental, quarrelsome, and a sour loser
- His instinctive nature can take him over

Demeter and Poseidon:
Living on Fertile Ground

My bounty is as boundless as the sea,
My love as deep. The more I give to thee,
The more I have, for both are infinite.

– WILLIAM SHAKESPEARE, *ROMEO AND JULIET* LL.2. 133–135

The Poseidon man and the Demeter woman fuel each other's creativity and sexuality, and help each other grow. Between them they bring together the two fundamental elements, earth and water. Water needs to be contained and given shape by the earth, and the earth needs water to become fertile and support life. She needs to receive so she can keep on giving – to him, to the family and to everything she does. He needs a safe haven where his emotions can be expressed and find release, and he finds it with her.

One man described his Demeter woman this way: 'She is my calm, she is like a field of anemones where I find my refuge. Sometimes as I lie beside her I let her see what I carefully conceal from everyone else, my momentary cowardice, and I like to think she keeps nothing from me. What haunts me disappears when I am with her. She might be in the kitchen cooking, and I'll be in my study writing, yet I'll feel her with me and be happy.'

Psychotherapy pioneer Sigmund Freud expressed similar feelings about his wife, Martha Bernays. During their four-year courtship he revealed his insecurities, his fears, his victories in love letters to her, holding back nothing. 'If today were to be my last on earth and someone asked me how I had fared, he would be told by me that in spite of everything – poverty, long struggle for success, little favour among men, oversensitivity, nervousness and worries – I have nevertheless been happy simply because of the anticipation of one day having you to myself and of the certainty that you love me. I have always been frank with you, haven't I? I haven't even made use of the license usually granted to a person of the other sex of showing you my best side. . . . I want nothing but to have you and to have you as you are.'

In the presence of a Demeter woman who loves him, the Poseidon man can harness his intense emotional energy, much as the way the banks of a river contain and direct the flow of water. He is safe to unfold, to explore, to go deeper, to engage his highly creative nature, and to mature. The Demeter woman brings an unconditionality to their relationship and a lack of criticism. She is totally accepting of him, his emotional ups and downs, and knows how to handle him. Even if they are young, she will still mother him, and he will love and respect her for it. He can go out and work and support them financially, and he feels secure that she is there, solid and committed.

It is very important for her to find in him a place where she is totally received, a place where her feminine power can be held. She is enlivened by his creative imagination. He is full of new ideas and feelings, and she is stirred and stimulated by him. He cherishes and appreciates her, and she feels she can keep giving because he recharges her. He protects her and will often say no for her sake when she doesn't know where to stop. He is the one who insists on time for them to be alone together, since her mothering nature will always want to include others. He relishes her body and loves making love to her. He sees in her the primordial mother earth that he worships, and she takes him in body, mind and soul. In the myth, Demeter and Poseidon take the form of horses – powerful, earthy, sexual and instinctive – when they mate. The Demeter/Poseidon partners merge with each other, but unlike Hades and Persephone, who get lost in each other, they merge only to resurface even fuller.

This relationship has the potential to outlast adversities. Once this couple makes the commitment to each other, they just get on with making their life together work. They are both elemental, and when they find each other, they bond. They honour that bond, and out of it comes a third entity, their relationship. The relationship itself is almost their child, and they care for and nurture it. It can be the foundation for wonderful, creative projects or bodies of work that can benefit many other people.

If the Poseidon man is not acknowledged by the world for who he is, he will feel unworthy and his masculine self-image will suffer. If he doesn't have work where he can express his rich, emotional creative nature, he will feel like a king without a kingdom. He will withdraw and shut down. Or he might take it out on his family, becoming angry, abusive and venting his feelings on his partner or their children. He may try to dominate her and can be sexually demanding. In either case, she suffers. It is like the earth trying to give new growth and meeting either drought or flood. She will be enraged when the rhythm of her productivity is blocked, but because she is not a confrontational woman, she is likely to withdraw and try to avoid him rather than fight. Unless he is prepared to do some inner work, he can be a great challenge to live with. It takes the goddess's strength to handle a man like this and not get depressed but to keep going.

If the Demeter woman moves more deeply into her role as a mother, her Aphrodite nature may recede. She might lose interest in romance and being a lover, especially if he has withdrawn or become abusive. He may want to have her for himself more often, while she is becoming increasingly devoted to their children. If he is not prepared to join her by stepping into the role of the family man, they may find themselves even further separated. Their relationship is not being fed and it begins to sicken.

My father had a lot of the negative aspects of the Poseidon man. He developed an addiction to gambling on horse races – how appropriate for Poseidon! – and when he lost, which was most of the time, he would come home all dark and brooding, and we knew to leave him alone. He was looking for his power in the wrong places. What he wanted was to express his adventurous self and have fun, and he wanted to do things his way. My mother wanted to raise her children, and she expected him to be the family man and do his part. Their separation was inevitable. My father was devastated, hurt and lonesome after the separation. He had lost his safe harbour, the family structure that had given him an anchor. He missed this in his life, even though when he had it, he had not taken care of it.

When I look back on my parents' lives, I can see the patterns in their lives so clearly. I also see how men can get so lost in their lower nature. Their identities can be wrapped up in sexuality, in self-image, in achievement. They have no reference for accessing their feminine, receptive nature, their heart, their authentic self, which is nevertheless there all along, underneath the turbulence. It is relatively easy for us women, living in a male-dominated culture, to access our masculine, assertive nature. It is demonstrated in the culture all around us. As we break free of seeing men as our solutions, as we discover our limitations and learn to honour ourselves, we can help the men in our lives evolve. It is not a matter of fixing or saving; rather, it is a matter of holding the reference point for another way of being for the man. When we own our power and bring that to our partner and our relationship, change does happen.

When Demeter lost her daughter, Persephone, she took on Zeus, king of the gods and her daughter's father. She stood firm in her truth and refused to back down. When Lysistrata in Aristophanes' comedy *Lysistrata* wanted to stop the Peloponnesian War, she directed the older women of Athens to seize the sacred precincts of the Acropolis and asked all the women of Greece to swear an oath that they would refuse sex with the men until peace was declared. Ultimately, the men conceded.

There are moments when the women are the ones to reach deeper and higher and bring light. Sometimes, if we simply hold what we know silently, with the strength and compassion of the earth herself, we extend an invitation for the man to shift. Collectively, we as women must hold a higher vision for both women and men. After all, it was Ariadne who gave Theseus the ball of string as he entered the labyrinth to slay the Minotaur. She told him to unwind it as he entered so he could trace his way out again. Theseus was willing and strong and capable of slaying the Minotaur, but he still needed a woman's help to get out of the labyrinth. Ariadne loved Theseus, so she helped him. The feminine often holds the key to the male's freedom – the feminine inside of him, if he can access it, but if he cannot, then we as women reflect it for him from outside himself.

Katie and Gay: A Commitment to Love

Love is the only thing you get more of by giving it away.

– TOM WILSON

Kathryn and Gay Hendricks, whose story is featured in their book, *Conscious Heart,* have an extraordinary relationship, a marriage that has lasted twenty-three years and is getting better all the time. What makes it extraordinary is their commitment to themselves and the way they honour themselves and each other by being willing to tell the truth at all times and at all costs. They have found the key to making their relationship work and have shared it with thousands of people all over the world through their books, seminars and private practice.

Gay has the Poseidon man's amazing willingness to feel all his emotions, the positive *and* the negative, fully. He is also blessed with an Apollonian rationality, a capacity to use his intellect to sort out his feelings and not be sunk by them. One day, when he had finished his academic studies in psychology and was getting ready to begin teaching, he came to a moment of truth. He opened up to his spirit and asked, 'What do I need to know or experience to give me unshakable confidence in my ability to transform myself in every moment?' When we ask with a willing heart and an open mind, the answer comes, and Gay's answer came loud and clear: 'Let yourself feel deeply, let yourself open up to who you truly are, and you will have the unity you seek. If you simply feel and express what is unarguably authentic, you will always be grounded in a space of integrity.' And the answer continued: 'The real problem is that you don't love yourself and the world exactly as it is. Every moment is an opportunity to expand in love; your job is to love yourself and all your experiences as they are, then make new choices from that space of love.'

Gay took this message as his personal credo and lived by it. He allowed all his feelings to come to life inside of him, and his Poseidon aspect was comfortable giving him permission to feel. What surfaced revealed much that he had hidden from himself. Rivers of sadness and fear from childhood were all given expression. It took courage but it was worth it because in the process he built trust in himself. He announced to his then girlfriend that he wanted a relationship of 100 per cent honesty, each of them taking full responsibility for their feelings and being committed to finding positive resolutions without quarrelling. Since she wasn't prepared for engaging at that level of openness, he ended the relationship then and there. He declared to himself that either he would have a committed, transparent, loving relationship or he would spend his life growing and expanding on his own.

It was at this point that he met Katie. A graduate student in one of his classes, she had been on a parallel path of growth and life-enhancement. She had left an unsupportive marriage and was raising her son, Chris, on her own, living her Demeter archetype to the fullest. 'Chris was my primary relationship, the one I protected and nurtured with every faculty I possessed. . . . Until Gay there had been no choice. Chris was the hub. . . . I had consolidated my early reading experiences into a personal comic-book version of Superwoman: the heroine who can do everything and still be feminine and totally responsive to her mate's every need. My fierce independence contained a trap, though. I was raising Chris, maintaining a private practice in movement therapy, going to graduate school, cleaning the house, making gourmet meals and sewing original creations – all without looking too closely at what I really wanted. . . . Gradually I learned that I could ask for what I wanted and could learn from that choice. Each one of my relationship decisions, even the steps backward, led me closer to the moment in that graduate school class when Gay and I recognised each other and I came home.' They described their first meeting as a moment of essence recognition.

There was a lot to work out as they moved in together –

the practicalities of life with two teenage kids, blending two families' finances, adjusting to each other's habits and learning how to express all their feelings and listen with no judgment. They found out that the routine demands of everyday life were the biggest barriers to embracing essence. Their relationship worked better when they remembered to nurture it by doing things like taking walks or bike rides together, meditating or dancing, and communicating their feelings. One of their fundamental commitments was to fully express their creativity. With Gay's encouragement, Katie let go of structured ways of doing life and learned to honour her impulse to create. She began writing poetry and publishing books of her own. Their explorations into how to tend to each other and honour their truth in the moment became the basis of their work together, Conscious Loving, about which they wrote books and conducted workshops, teaching thousands of people these skills. Fifteen years into their marriage these were two people who were blossoming and helping others to blossom as well.

Our myths have an uncanny way of revisiting us until we are totally free of them. Responding to the escalating demands of their work and life together, Katie had once again become the superwoman. Caught up in her mothering role and her old habit of doing everything and doing all of it well, she ran the institute they had created, managed their private practice, organised the workshops and took care of Gay. Her responsibilities crowded out time for creative expression, and she was neglecting the joy of her femininity as well. She had gained fifteen extra pounds, and their sexual relationship was less and less active. It was hard to be aroused by the mother energy, Gay admitted to me.

Gay, on the other hand, was running on automatic pilot. He had become a well-known therapist and an expert in his field with many books published. They had enough money, the children were launched into their own lives, the business was successful and they had wonderful friends all over the world. The work was expanding, but he had lost touch with his aliveness and creativity. Outwardly everything was going great, but he could feel the subtle difference. He was entering his fifties, a critical decade when men and women face the choice of either renewing themselves or stagnating. It is a crossroads – the place of Hermes, the messenger and mystical god – where one must choose between expanding and reinventing oneself, on the one hand, and contracting and yielding to the aging process, on the other. It is a time when people may have an affair, wishing to experience their youth again – anything to avoid facing the glaring fact that they are not immortal.

It was at a friend's birthday party that Gay was struck by Eros's arrow. There was 'Aphrodite', radiant, slender and curvy, moving on the dance floor, her long hair shimmering in the soft light. She was Kristin, a former student of Gay and Katie's who was beginning her doctoral studies in the field of body-centred psychotherapy, Gay's field. At the sight of her, he said, 'Every cell in my body felt alive. . . . It was as if I had been living at 50 per cent when a sudden shift took me to 150 per cent. . . . It felt like some part of me was waking up at long last. It certainly had a sexual component, although it reached into areas of myself that felt spiritual as well.' Because of his commitment to telling the truth about his feelings as soon as they happened, he approached Kristin and told her what he was feeling. The attraction turned out to be mutual. Then he called Katie over from across the room and told her what he was experiencing.

Katie was understandably hurt and fearful. Her eyes moistened as she gestured toward Kristin and said, 'How can I compete with that?' Katie told Gay that if he had sexual relations with Kristin, she would leave him.

What unfolded in the next three months was the extraordinary process of two people committed to the creative spirit, to love, and to telling the truth. Gay wanted to allow himself to experience the new aliveness he felt with Kristin, and he wanted to feel those feelings totally and not deny or suppress them. He didn't necessarily want to take Kristin to bed, but he wanted to be around her, and she wanted to be around him. He didn't want to exclude Katie from his feelings; rather, he wanted to share the process with her as it went on. Gay told me, 'I knew that if I followed my feelings I would not be destroyed nor my relationship with Katie. I trusted myself in my feelings, and I knew the world wouldn't collapse.'

Katie, too, was going through one of the most intense processes of her life. She saw how she had merged her identity with Gay's, how she had given over creative parts of herself to him so she could take on extra responsibilities, how she had stopped listening to herself and forgotten to set boundaries and sometimes say no. She realised that it was time for her to find out how to be alone. She had never been alone before. Like so many women, she had always been with someone and been defined by her relationship with them. She had to face her fear of aloneness, her fear that the man she loved might have a sexual relationship with another woman. She saw that she could not control him. She had to let go and love him just the way he chose to be. She faced all the collective issues around the ways women have been devalued, and she kept giving them voice because they needed to come out. Often she felt like she was dying, and she was. An old part of her consciousness was breathing its last breath. Katie was both Demeter, waiting for the reemergence of a part of her feminine self, and Persephone, whose life had abruptly collapsed on itself, shaking her out of the world she knew so a new reality could take its place.

It is only when we give up the world as we have known it that we can find our true self. Then the spirit in us opens up and breathes again. Katie was writing poetry with a new passion to express all the new feelings:

> What remains of love?
> When the web of knowing and holding
> Shimmers and sinks into the vast pool.
> A mutation glimmers in the depths
> That is still unformed
> And yearning with a lidless eye.

Gay asked Katie to let go of trying to control any aspect of his life, and once she realised that she couldn't control him no matter how she reacted, a sense of liberation emerged in her body and a new self emerged, not yet defined but free. She examined the negative filters through which she saw herself – the perfection that was expected of her as a little girl and how little room there had been for mistakes. She had always been expected to show the polished result, but never the process of growth. Like a devoted surgeon, where she saw fear she removed it. As she explains, she would feel paralysed at first as the fear surfaced, then she would let herself feel it and express it, and then she would take some creative action and feel elated and free. She took leaps toward her freedom. Her Artemis spirit was awakening, and she went kayaking and skydiving in Alaska.

'I saw that I have my life and can accomplish the kind of magic that I had always thought Gay owned,' Katie said. 'I realised that for a year I had been full of power and not

owning it, not fully stepping into sourcing responsibility.'
She saw how her devoted persona of the caretaker, her
Demeter, and Gay's critic, his stern Poseidon, had inter-
locked and that this crisis was the final jolt that could move
her out of that persona once and for all. The extra physical
weight fell off her within two weeks as that persona melted
from her. She felt new energy and aliveness in her body and
a new response to her life, to her creativity and to being
fully responsible for her life independent of Gay. It was both
scary and enlivening.

Meanwhile, Gay was having his own epiphanies. He
realised that his sexual attraction to Kristin was really a
waking up to new levels of creativity. Since his reference
was sexuality, his Poseidon archetype had attracted a
beautiful nymph so he could awaken a dormant part of
himself. He had felt that the wild, carefree part of him
was dying, replaced by the father figure who knew everything. His interaction with Kristin was a wake-up call to
the creative part within that had been submerged. He had
to dive even deeper to parts of his creative nature that
were as yet unknown.

One night during this time, as he was sitting in his
study, Gay made a pact to himself and the universe: 'From
now on creativity would be my highest priority. I decided
to turn myself over to its full expression through me. If my
relationship with Katie was humming with love and good
energy I would assume that my relationship with my creativity was good. If my relationship with her was feeling
disharmonious, I would regard it as a symptom that I was
out of harmony with my creativity. Everything began to
shift in my body and spirit. . . . A fresh new field of energy
began to pulsate in me, a new and vaster spaciousness than
I had felt before. It was something I could feel and see at

the same time. I felt a benign breeze coursing through my body. . . . Along with the breeze I could see more radiance and light inside me.'

Eight years have passed since that major event in their lives, and the happy outcome has surprised them as much as anyone else. Their relationship has become fuller because each of them feels an enhanced connection to their source of creativity. They are more deeply committed to each other. Their work has continued to grow, they have written more books together and they have bought a house in Ojai, California, where they feel for the first time they have found their real home.

To quote Shakespeare, 'A little madness in the spring is even good for the king'.

Demeter Speaks

When I gazed into the eyes of Demeter, goddess of
   the earth,
Mother of us all,
I saw oceans of love and compassion.
And then I saw such sorrow that her tears
Flowed in all the rivers on the earth.
So I knelt before her like a child
Who loves her mother so and asked that she put her
   hands upon my head
And tell how I might serve her,
For I had never seen such love and sorrow in one.
And this is what she said:
This earth is under my protection, she is my heart.
I love her as a mother loves her only child.
I have no other like her, she is my only daughter,

Every branch in every tree
And every fruit in every seed
And every blade of grass and every field and flower
And every river and all the oceans
And every root that grows deep beneath the earth
I love with all my heart.
I rejoice when things grow,
When I see men take my wheat, make bread,
And feed themselves and their children.
The more they take, the more I give.
That is my nature: life giver, selfless caretaker,
Mother of my children.
And now, my daughter, the earth itself has been
    abducted,
Raped and polluted,
My heart is ripped by what men have done,
My eyes weep for what they have seen.
My children are hungry and they are starved.
In the midst of plenty there is famine.
I weep but I am angry, angry with the cruelty of
    man.
What can I do to serve you?
Be kind
Be gentle
Be caring
Be watchful
Be smart.
Educate yourself and learn how your mother is
    abused
And then take action.
And then her radiant, golden face
With long, golden hair
Became the emaciated face and wrinkled form

Of a withered old woman.
And I knew
That every tree that had been cut
And every field that had been sprayed
And every ache and every cry of a starved child
Had gone into her body and caused her heart to ache.
And I wept with her. . . .
Then so gently she gave me her hand,
Called me to stand, and said
Let's start.
Make this earth whole again,
One seed at a time.
Honour the ground you walk on.
Bless all that you see and touch,
So we can make this earth holy again.

Chapter 10

DIONYSUS,
CELEBRATING LIFE

He who knows the power of the dance dwells in God.

— RUMI

I have left Dionysus for last because he stands alone in relationship to life itself as a being of mirth and ecstasy who
gives us permission to break away from the confines of our
existence and experience the magical dimension of another
reality where the freedom of our spirit lies. All of us, both
men and women, must embrace him if we want to keep our
joy alive, if we want to experience life as a celebration rather
than an obligation. In ancient Greece he was the god of
wine, ecstatic dance and theatre. He was known as the god
who liberates us from troubles and cleanses our souls. He is
the god who saves us when we feel abandoned and depressed. As the poet Rumi says:

You moan, 'She left me.' 'He left me.'
Twenty more will come.
Be empty of worrying. . . .
Why do you stay in prison
When the door is so wide open?
Move outside the tangle of fear-thinking.
Flow down and down in always
Widening rings of being.

Dionysus stands at the opposite end of the archetypal spectrum from balanced, rational Apollo and declares, 'Everything in excess!' At ancient Delphi they were both worshipped – Dionysus through his theatre and Apollo in his temple – because the Greeks knew that both the rational and the irrational must be honoured. Albert Einstein recognised this truth: 'The intuitive mind is a sacred gift and the rational mind is a faithful servant. We have created a society that honours the servant and has forgotten the gift.'

He comes to wake us up, to loosen our grip when we are reluctant to let go. He helps us move from inertia to creativity and rediscover our enthusiasm for life. I have a friend, a psychotherapist, who used to say that the best remedy for depression is dancing, and she would ask her clients to dance out their angst and their issues; it is hard to be depressed when you are out of breath. Friedrich Nietzsche said, 'We should consider every day lost on which we have not danced at least once.' And the Sufi dervishes say, 'When you dance, all the stars and the planets and the endless universes dance around that still point. The heavens respond and the invisible kingdoms join in the dance.'

Every culture honours the Dionysian spirit in one form or another. In the town of Bunyol in Valencia, Spain, there is an annual tomato festival where thousands of people take to the streets, throwing ripe tomatoes at each other until everyone is drenched with tomato pulp. It is quite a sight! The Carnival of Rio de Janeiro and the Mardi Gras in New Orleans are famous celebrations in which people take to the streets to express their craziness – drinking and dancing with strangers to wild music, wearing masks and costumes, and wearing and throwing colourful beads. Everything is permitted that day.

Modern Greeks honour Dionysus in the *tavernas,* where they gather at night, singing and dancing and following the age-old custom of breaking plates. They let go of the worries and burdens of the day and share in the joy of the moment. I remember taking some of my friends visiting from America to a *taverna,* and as the night progressed and my Greek friends got a little tipsier and a little happier, my American friends asked, 'How are they ever going to go to work to-morrow?' 'Don't worry,' I said, 'they'll have more energy be-cause they have made their hearts happy.'

The movie *Zorba the Greek* is a story of an Apollo man learning from the 'crazy wisdom' of a Dionysus. While wait-ing for the boat to embark from Athens for Crete, earthy, free-spirited Zorba befriends Basil, the English writer and says, 'Take me with you.' 'Why?' asks Basil. Zorba replies, 'You think too much and ask such sensible questions. Would a man ever do anything without a why?' Gradually, the two men bond. When Basil is reluctant to visit the widow he is enamoured of, Zorba encourages him: 'To be alive is to be able to undo your belt and look for trouble.' Later, when Zorba dances ecstatically until he drops to the ground, Basil asks him what happened, and Zorba replies, 'When a man is full, what can he do but burst? When my son died, every-body cried and I danced. Everyone thought Zorba was mad. But it was dancing, only the dancing, that stopped the pain.'

At the end of the movie, when Basil is contemplating leaving, Zorba tells him, 'You have everything except one thing: madness. A man needs a little bit of madness or else he never dares cut the rope and be free.' Then Basil asks Zorba to teach him to dance. They break into a joyful dance; the Dionysian spirit has finally broken through the Apollonian form.

Of course, the ecstatic Dionysian spirit, when it is not channelled into creativity, can turn and become violent and destructive. This double nature of the god is symbolised in the double nature of wine, which has the power to release our inhibitions and bring us pleasure but can also destroy us. Alcohol is called 'spirit' for good reason. Often when people drink they are really trying to connect with their own spirit and experience their soul's freedom, but it's at the risk of becoming addicted and losing their freedom rather than gaining it.

Dionysus was the child of Zeus and the mortal Semele, who died while the child was still in her womb. Zeus rescued him and sewed him into his thigh, where he remained, protected, until he was full term. Vengeful Hera pursued and tried to destroy this offspring of yet another of Zeus's escapades, but he was always protected and saved by Zeus, who had made him immortal. His tutor, Silenus, taught him the secrets of nature and how to make wine. He is often portrayed wearing a wreath of vine leaves and dancing wildly with the nymphs.

Dionysus generously rewarded those who honoured him, and he punished those who ignored him by driving them mad and making them do irrational acts. In Euripides' play *The Bacchae*, King Pentheus, who worships the reasonable Apollo and despises Dionysus's excessive ways, arrests the god, and it costs him his life. In the traditions surrounding

Dionysus, groups of *maenads,* or *bacchae,* women who took part in the god's orgiastic rites, are described as falling into a state of ecstasy, a sort of divine madness, through frenzied dance. They would run through the woods and if they came across a wild animal, would tear it apart and eat its flesh, believing that this brought them in contact with the god, who Zeus had once changed into a goat. In the play, the *bacchae* end up tearing apart Pentheus, who was watching with curiosity to see what took place in those rituals. The women included his mother, Agave, who, once she was out of trance, realised with horror that she had torn apart her own son. The god shouts, 'Too late you had learnt to know me.' When we don't recognise Dionysus, the price we pay is that we are psychologically torn apart.

The Dionysian man today is the rock star who induces thousands of people to dance and sing and go wild at a concert. He is the man who parties into the wee hours of the night and sleeps the day away. He is the man who seeks altered states of consciousness as a way of finding ecstasy or escaping reality, forgetting that he is in a human body that will suffer his excesses. He is also the director, actor, opera singer, or dancer who has learned to channel the Dionysian creative genius into a production or a performance. He feels the fire of the god so intensely in his body that he must find a creative outlet for it. His work can transport us out of our human condition into another reality, the realm of the god. His yearning to tap into another reality can lead him to become a great mystic, drunk with the divine, like the twelfth-century poet Rumi.

The man who embodies the Dionysus archetype has been touched by the madness of the god and embodies the god's wild forces, which our Apollonian Western civilisation tries to keep at bay. He is the one who breaks all the rules, who has a great appetite for the extreme and even dangerous, who lives on the edge. In the words of musician and actor Oscar Levant, 'There is a fine line between genius and insanity, I have erased this line.' He doesn't care about security or social approval or worldly success. He seeks the emotional high, the experience of being alive in all his senses. Because his expression lies in the field of creative arts, if he is talented he may feel that things should just happen for him, that the world should recognise him and give him special treatment. Sometimes the world does, and his talents manifest and explode and he can become immensely successful and famous, like Mick Jagger or David Bowie. If, however, the opportunities don't come, he can end up playing his guitar in the garage with his buddies, taking abusive substances, resentful that his specialness goes unrecognised.

His intense erotic nature can lead him from affair to affair and leave a trail of wounded hearts behind him. He is a passionate, uninhibited lover who fully abandons himself to lovemaking in the moment and can show a woman the way to ecstasy. A woman can become addicted to such a man. His sensuality and love of life can draw her in. Because his focus is on the experience more than the relationship, he can participate fully without necessarily making a personal connection with his partner. She may then find herself having to live with his impulsiveness and unpredictability. This is not a man you can control in any way. He comes and goes as he pleases.

The Dionysus man's sensuality and spontaneity will appeal to an Aphrodite woman. She can match his erotic passion. Together they might be consumed by their urges and have no boundaries. Seeking wild adventure and the next high, they run the risk of burning out. The Persephone woman will also be attracted to this man. She can feel at home with his ups and downs. Wherever he is going, she'll pack her bags and go with him without a second thought. They can have a 'truly madly deeply' love affair or a long-term relationship, but they would be wise to see that it doesn't lead them both into the underworld. They must keep one foot on the earth – or a toe, at least.

It was Dionysus who saved Ariadne after Theseus abandoned her. Ariadne loved Theseus and had helped him find his way out of the labyrinth after killing the Minotaur. Theseus took her with him on his return to Athens, promising to marry her. But along the way he abandoned her on the island of Naxos. Dionysus fell in love with her, took her away in his chariot and loved her. He is the god who can bring us back to life when we are bereft. He reminds us that life is worth living and should be lived to the fullest.

Dionysus comes alive in us – both men and women – when we sing and dance, when we give up our constricted self-images and linear thinking, throw caution to the winds and remember our joy. He takes us out of our settled existence and enchants us with out-of-the-ordinary feelings and thoughts. When we feel oppressed by life, it is because we have exiled Dionysus. When we feel our relationships are monotonous, it is because we have buried the god's spontaneity. He will find ways to remind us of his existence so we will unearth him. Dionysus is the god of here and now, bringing us back to the moment.

Pick your favourite music, and dance in honour of this god. Without him, life is dry and dull. With him, we experience the rapture and the vitality of our being.

EPILOGUE

As I was writing this book I had to let go of my precon-
ceptions about the gods and goddesses and discover them
anew. They took me deeper into myself and gifted me with
new insights. Gods and goddesses tend to do that. But one
thing has not changed – my passion about how important
these archetypes and myths are for us today.

As we make the gods and goddesses our own, we must
look to them as guides to our freedom. They offer us new
ways of looking at ourselves and our relationships. Embrace
them; they help us dissolve the labels and limitations we tend
to put on ourselves. And as we discover other aspects of ourselves that we can nurture, we will realise how many more
choices we have because we now control our destiny. We
often look at the glass as half empty or half full. But in reality
the glass is neither half empty nor half full. It is always full –
if not of water, then of air. So even in the hardest times, the
glass is always full.

We cannot seek to resolve our problems at the same

level where we created them. We must step up to a higher perspective where we can see the larger picture. The myths themselves show us solutions, for everything that happens to the gods and goddesses is a metaphor of what happens to us. When we are caught in a pattern, we cannot see beyond it. But when we connect our pattern to the myth, we can see the whole story. If we are trapped in the loneliness of our Persephone underworld, we may be unable to see what awaits us up on the surface world or to feel the love of our mother Demeter waiting for us. But the myth tells us that Persephone not only returns to the surface but becomes the master – queen – of her own underworld. Or, if we are caught in the jealousy and fury of the betrayed Hera and cannot see past our anger, justified as it might be. Hera's myth presents the possibility of returning to our source, renewing ourselves and finding our own power. As we fill out our archetypal stories, our view expands, and we find our freedom.

Relationship is the arena where all of this comes into play. Relationships are our teachers; they are the great universities of the heart. To succeed takes a willingness to change, to ask and listen, to let go and receive. Sometimes it takes a few relationships before we master the art of 'being together'. Margaret Mead, who was married three times, once said, 'All three of my marriages were great successes.' Or it may take a great deal of work within the same relationship as both partners grow. When Jungian psychotherapist Marion Woodman was asked how many times she had been married, she responded, 'Four times – to the same man,' because both she and her husband kept evolving.

The Greeks made a distinction between *eros,* erotic love, and *agape,* unconditional love. Our relationships often start with the infatuation of eros – we see our partner as a god, he sees us as a goddess. But at some point the first blush of eros goes. We begin to notice the flaws in our partner and the flaws in ourselves. As we accept each others' limitations, we tap into the agape love. Standing in this unconditional love, it is so much easier to face our shadow, the dark side of the archetypes. We pass through the underworld and up to the surface again. But we don't do it alone; there is the power of agape to accompany us. Our underworld doesn't scare us anymore because we know the way out. There is always a rope waving above our heads, available to us at a moment's request, ready to grab and lift ourselves out. Then a new level of love appears. We now have love and compassion for each others' humanness, for the struggles each has faced, for who each one of us truly is. We fall in love all over again with the whole person. This kind of love is a soulful eros, infused with agape. It is the stuff that glues the universe together, and it is real. It is in us always, no matter how difficult it is for us to discover it. We need both eros and agape. Without them we merely exist; with them we find joy and fulfilment.

We must unravel the myths and let the gods and goddesses become our allies. They will empower us by claiming the strengths and qualities hidden within us. Then we will see our partner and ourselves with new eyes, and agape and eros will permeate our life and become a reality for us.

BIBLIOGRAPHY

Amanpour, Christiane. Quotation from: www.la.utexas.edu/
chenry/usme/sp2001/roles/msg00067.html.

Anderson, Sherwood. *Love Letters: A Romantic Treasury*,
Philadelphia: Running Press, 1996.

Bolen, Jean Shinoda. *Goddesses in Everywoman: A New
Psychology of Women*. New York: Harper Perennial, 1984.

— Gods in Everyman: *A New Psychology of Men's Lives
and Loves*. New York: Harper & Row Publishers, 1989.

Brel, Jacques. 'Song of the Old Lovers'. Translation by Eric
Blau and Mort Shuman. Quotation from: home.tiscali.nl/
~phendr/gedichten/vieuxamants.html.

Campbell, Joseph, and Bill Moyers. *The Power of Myth*.
New York: Doubleday, 1988.

Churchill, Winston. Quotation from: www.quoteland.com/
library/speeches/Churchill.asp.

Freud, Sigmund. *Letters of Sigmund Freud*. Selected and
edited by Ernst L. Freud. New York: Dover, 1960.

Green, Laura, et al. *Reinventing Home: Six Working Women
Look at Their Home Lives*. New York: Plume, 1991.

Hendricks, Kathlyn, and Gay Hendricks. *The Conscious
Heart: Seven Soul-Choices That Inspire Creative Partnership*. New York: Bantam Books, 1999.

Ibsen, Henrik. *A Doll's House*. Adapted by Frank Guinness.
New York: Dramatist's Play Service, 1998.

Jung, C. G. *Memories, Dreams, Reflections*. Translated by
Richard and Clara Winston. Rev. ed. New York: Vintage
Books, 1989.

Kavafi. *Ithaka*. Adapted from translation by Edmund Keeley and Phillip Sherrard. Available at: ithaca.rice.edu/kz/Misc/Ithaka.html.

Lahr, Jane, and Lena Tabori. *Love: A Celebration in Art and Literature*. New York: Stuart Tabori and Chang, 1982.

Lawrence, D. H. *Women in Love*. New York: Penguin Books, 1976.

Mailer, Norman. *Of Women and Their Elegance*. New York: Simon & Schuster, 1980.

Mavromataki, Maria. *Greek Mythology and Religion*. Athens: Haïtalis, 1997.

Moore, Thomas. *The Soul of Sex*. New York: Harper Perennial, 1998.

Shakespeare, William. *William Shakespeare: The Complete Works*. New York: Gramercy, 1990.

Shaw, Bernard. *Candida*. New York: Samuel French, 1952.

— *Man and Superman*. London: Penguin Books, 1903.

Stassinopoulos, Agapi. *Conversations with the Goddesses: Revealing the Divine Power within You*. New York: Stewart, Tabori & Chang, 1999.

Stassinopoulos, Arianna, and Roloff Beny. *The Gods of Greece*. New York: Harry N. Abrams Inc. Publishers, 1983.

Wallerstein, Judith S., and Sandra Blakeslee. *The Good Marriage: How and Why Love Lasts*. New York: Warner Books, 1995.

Wells, Stanley, ed. *The Oxford Shakespeare: King Henry VIII*. New York: Oxford University Press, 1999.

Wilde, Oscar. *De Profundis*. New York: Vintage Books, 1964.

Woolger, Jennifer Barker, and Roger J. Woolger. *The Goddess Within: A Guide to the Eternal Myths That Shape Women's Lives*. New York: Fawcett Columbine, 1989.

Yalom, Marilyn. *History of the Wife*. New York: Harper-Collins Publishers, 2001.

ACKNOWLEDGMENTS

My thanks go to my dear friend John Morton who first planted the seed for this book. When talking about the goddesses he told me, 'Don't forget the gods.' I am grateful to my friend and mentor Jane Lahr, who encouraged me with the idea of this book as the natural follow-up to my book on the goddesses, and helped me water the seed.

My heartfelt thanks go to my Hermes agent, Harvey Klinger, who was the wind beneath my wings. He believed in this book right from the start. It would have never happened without him.

To my editor at Paraview Pocket Books, Patrick Huyghe, many thanks for his passion for the book, his patience as he extended my deadline, and his clarity all the way through.

Thanks to my friend Jean Houston, who read my material and encouraged me and found the perfect person to edit the book while I was writing it, the wonderful Carolyn Bond. Carolyn's Hestia calmness and patience together with her clear Athena eye for detail and her caring for the material made the writing process a most creative experience. My deepest thanks go to her.

So many dear friends contributed their personal stories and shared with me intimate details of how they made their relationships work. Others read and commented on chapters and offered suggestions and support. To all of them I am deeply grateful: Karen Oliver, Karen and Richard Powell, Frank and Katherine Price, Arielle Ford and Brian Hilliard, Phyllis Firak, Amelia Dallenbach, Faith Bethelard, Horatio

Fabiano, Joan Witkowski, Debbie Robins (my Athena cheerleader), Gay and Katie Hendricks, Jan Shepherd, Leigh Taylor Young, Nancy Evans, Seymour Wishman, Heide Banks, Hilary Tate, Florie Brizel, Richard Klein, Fran Lasker, Michael Hayes, Michael Gelb, Shelley Reid, Steve Small and Melinda Henneberger.

My thanks go also to Maricella Garcia, who always brings me so much joy and reminds me to dance; to John Roger, whose loving support is invaluable to me; to my sister, Arianna, who started her campaign for governor while this book was under deadline and showed me ways to keep writing and also be part of her campaign; and to Isabella and Christina, my beautiful nieces, who always fill my heart.

HOW HAVE

THE GODS AND GODDESSES

INFLUENCED YOUR RELATIONSHIPS?

If you have a story you would like to share about how your Gods and Goddesses have come into play, please send it to:

Agapi Stassinopoulos
1158 26th Street #428
Santa Monica, CA 90403

Or email it to: agapi@7goddesses.com

Please be sure to include your name, mailing address, and email address.

For further information about workshops,
speaking engagements and video tapes, visit my website:
www.sevengoddesses.com